KATHY DEGRAW
LAUREN DEBOER

SPEAK
LIFE

Prayer Declarations for Fertility, IVF, Pregnancy, Labor, Delivery, and Healthy Babies

K Advancement LLC

Speak Life

Scripture quotations are taken from The Holy Bible, Modern English Version (MEV), Copyright © 2014 by Military Bible Association. Published and distributed by Charisma House. Used by permission. All rights reserved.

Speak Life
Prayer Declarations for Fertility, IVF, Pregnancy, Labor, Delivery, and Healthy Babies

© 2026 Kathy DeGraw

ISBN: 979-8-9949398-0-2

K Advancement LLC
Kathy DeGraw Ministries
P.O. Box 65
Grandville, MI 49468

Book cover and Interior Layout: Tana Stephens
For cover creation, editing and formatting services
email: tstephens.kdministries@gmail.com

Dedication

To Levi: Our miracle baby who birthed this book! We praise and give thanks to the Lord for protecting you and bringing you into our lives!

Table of Contents

Opening Prophetic Word

What is a prophetic word? It is a word given by the Holy Spirit, through prayer, to a person. In a time of prayer, we can hear from the Holy Spirit. He can give us a word of encouragement. I, (Kathy), have started many of my books for years with a prophetic word intended for the reader. I sought the Lord for you in prayer, and this is what I heard. May it give you hope and peace!

Life, life in abundance, it is what I desire to give. I know some of you have waited, and some have longed, and let me tell you that I am the life-giver and life-sustainer. I desire to give life. I know you don't understand, and for some of you, the answer is simply that we live in a fallen world with hormone disruptors, environmental factors, and man-made things that prevent the life I desire to give. Have hope. I do desire to give life, and I desire to give it to you, not just everyone else. Your waiting and your prayers are not in vain. Read my book, the Bible. It is all about life, children, love, and family. I desire to give you the desires of your heart, so while you are waiting and grieving for the moment when you finally hold that child, have hope. Your waiting is not in vain. I am the life-giver, and although some will never experience the life I want to create, I still desire to give it. Therefore, keep praying, keep believing, keep hoping, and have faith that I will grant you the desires of your heart.

Introduction

Years ago, I said that I could relate to most women in everything regarding infertility, pregnancy, and childbearing issues. I didn't realize that I was actually prophesying about the future when I spoke those words aloud. I didn't know that very prophecy was coming true until we were two-thirds of the way through this book, and those words came back to me.

I am so glad I spoke those words, and I am truly glad that prophecy is finally coming true. I do not regret what I have gone through or experienced if it can help you. A scripture that has been pivotal over the past several months is, all things work together for good, (Romans 8:28). As I will write about later, I don't always believe that it is working together for our personal good, but it does work together for God's good. He can use what we go through to help others.

Over the years, I have suffered infertility and a partial molar pregnancy, which resulted in the loss of my twins, Nathan and Katelyn. I was then told not to get pregnant for a year because it could cause cancer. In labor, I had a forceps delivery where my baby was resuscitated twice and put in the neonatal intensive care unit NICU. The use of the forceps resulted in my not being able to walk well for weeks following the delivery. I also left the hospital without my baby, which was emotionally grueling and eventually led to me choosing two elective C-sections so that my next two babies wouldn't get stuck during labor. When I was on the operating table for the delivery of my last child, it was decided for me that I shouldn't have any more children. If I did, my uterus, scar tissue and body would not be able to handle one minute of labor.

I've gone from a child not knowing how to suck, to taking a bottle, to wanting to breastfeed, to not being able to breastfeed, to praying and having a baby that was the perfect breast feeder. I've been through a lot, and I feel like I can relate to a lot of people, but I never imagined God would use it this way.

Lauren and I birthed this book out of her high-risk pregnancy and the birth of her latest child. When the diagnosis wasn't promising, we warred, fought, prayed and believed Jesus above every ultrasound and doctor's report. We absolutely refused to speak out about what they said could happen. I didn't even tell my husband, Lauren's dad, because I didn't want negativity, doubt, or talk about it that could release word curses or anything else in the spiritual atmosphere or natural manifestations. The Bible says, "You will have whatever you say, speak to your mountain and it will be removed, and death and life are in the power of the tongue" (Prov. 18:21). We take those words literally.

Ask and it will be given to you; seek and you will find; knock and it will be opened to you.

— Matthew 7:7

For truly I say to you, whoever says to this mountain, "Be removed and be thrown into the sea," and does not doubt in his heart, but believes that what he says will come to pass, he will have whatever he says.

— Mark 11:23

During her latest delivery, I was called up as emotional support. I had been her prayer partner, and I needed to pray for what was happening and assist with medical care and decisions. Thankfully, her story had a happy ending, but during her labor, I had to ask her Christian doctor how to pray specifically for the delivery and for her baby. I asked her to tell me explicitly, and I wrote down every instruction. We knew in that delivery room that God was not only birthing a baby, but a book. The kids even said, "Are you going to write another book?" Well, isn't that what writers do? They take what they have experienced and use it to author a book that can help others.

It became a passion for Lauren and me to help other women, men, and grandparents. It isn't just about giving life to moms and dads, but it is about giving their parents a chance to be grandparents. I never knew the joy it would bring to my heart to have grandchildren. As I was writing this book, I was so grieved for those who will never know that joy. I was also grieved for those who need in vitro fertilization (IVF) and those who have been diagnosed with polycystic ovary syndrome (PCOS). God burdened our hearts, for these people.

It is our deepest hope and prayer that you will produce life and produce it abundantly and healthily. Friends, if I may, I want to share some testimonies from people I have prayed for over the years who now have not only children but multiple children.

- A woman who had blocked fallopian tubes has since been able to have three children without medical intervention.
- One lady was told she would only ovulate every 9 months and became pregnant 6 weeks after I laid hands on her and prayed for her, and she now has 5 children.
- A lady who spotted for a full week during her pregnancy received prayer, and instead of miscarrying, she made it to full term with that baby and now has 3 children.
- A lady who had struggled with infertility for 7 years got pregnant only a year after we prayed for her, and she now has 4 children.
- Another woman received three negative diagnoses after going to the doctor, but later became pregnant 6-8 weeks after I laid hands on her and broke off the doctors' words and called forth life.

I have had many testimonies and pictures sent in over the years from people who tried and couldn't, or doctors said it was impossible, but God said it was possible.

I want to pray those same life-producing prayers over you. If you bought this book through my ministry, it included a prayer cloth that was anointed with holy anointing oil and prayed over for you to receive those same miracles. If you purchased this book on Amazon, we would love to give you a prayer cloth. You can receive a free prayer cloth by sending a S.A.S.E. to KDM, PO Box 65, Grandville, MI 49468.

> If you prefer, you can support our ministry and help cover the cost of the prayer cloths by purchasing them online at kathydegrawministries.org or by scanning the QR code.

I encourage you to get yourself some anointing oil from my Amazon store page and anoint your womb (your lower pelvis externally) daily and call forth life. Speak out the scriptures on birth and on how God intends for us to have children and pray the positive declarations that call forth life throughout this book.

> Kathy's Amazon Store Page
>
> Scan QR Code

How Use This Book

This is a book full of prayer declarations for many different situations. Unfortunately, we cannot possibly include everything or every condition. I encourage you to highlight the prayers that apply to you or put sticky notes on the pages you need to read. Don't concern yourself with every prayer. Go to the sections you marked and pray those prayers repeatedly. Trust God for your baby. Pray with faith. These prayers are meant to be spoken aloud, not prayed in your mind. You are taking authority over your body to align with pregnancy, and we need to command it on what to do. Keep expecting God to protect and move on your behalf. He is the giver and sustainer of life. We are praying for you!

He will love you and bless you and multiply you. He will also bless the fruit of your womb and the fruit of your ground, your grain and your wine and your oil, the increase of your herds and the young of your flock in the land that he swore to your fathers to give you.

— Deuteronomy 7:13

Speak Life! It is the most appropriate title! Lauren and I are praying for you and expecting you to join us in praying and speaking life over your womb! This book will take a bit to go through, so let's get you started right away on speaking life over your womb!

I love anointing oil! If you don't know, anointing oil is olive oil with essential oils or other raw materials mixed, put in a bottle, and prayed over for protection, healing, freedom, consecration, and many other things. It is biblical to use anointing oil. I have a ministry that distributes anointing oil and teaches about it on YouTube. I have been healed many times using anointing oil.

13

You can get a free downloadable PDF on the Biblical Usage and Understanding of Anointing Oil by scanning the QR code.

You don't have to use anointing oil. However, since I have seen the power of prayer, standing in agreement with you, and the healing power of Jesus manifest through it, I encourage you to use it.

How to Use Anointing Oil

Place a small amount of anointing oil on your finger and then touch your abdomen and speak life into your womb. You can pray for anything you feel led to pray. If you are ever given a bad diagnosis or a concerning medical report while pregnant, anoint yourself and rebuke that report. Speak life and health over your baby. You can anoint yourself daily with anointing oil while you are pregnant or while you are trying to be healed of infertility. You don't have to anoint your abdomen if you don't want to. You can pray and anoint yourself anywhere on your body.

When purchasing anointing oil and using it during pregnancy, frankincense and myrrh are generally safe (see your health practitioner for confirmation). We have frankincense and myrrh anointing oil, mixed with olive oil, on our Amazon store page, along with unscented anointing oil. Cinnamon is not safe during pregnancy. Therefore, please do not order the Exodus 30 blend on the store page.

Order Anointing Oil that Kathy's ministry has made and prayed over on Amazon. Do not order Exodus 30 blends while pregnant. All anointing oils include a standard prayer cloth, but not a baby prayer cloth.

Scan the QR code if you would like to purchase a pregnancy, IVF, or baby prayer cloth. We anoint all of these with oil and pray for you!

You can place the prayer cloth on your abdomen, pray, and speak life. It is the prayer of agreement you are receiving in the prayer cloth. It is us praying over them, anointing them, and speaking life, conception, health, and healing over them for you.

PRAYER

God, we come to You right now and ask that You help touch every person who reads this book. Let their hearts and minds be open to what You want to do in their lives. Give them courage and strength to pray these prayers and to have trust in You for their circumstance.

God, I thank You that my body is being healed as I read this book. I thank You for the blessings that will flow from my life as a result of praying these prayers. I thank You for the healing that is coming forth, in Jesus' name.

PRAYER DECLARATIONS

I anoint my baby in the name of Jesus! I say he/she will be full of life, health and strength. This pregnancy is going to be the easiest pregnancy ever. I will be full of strength and energy!

I speak life into my womb, life is coming forth, in Jesus' name! No weapon formed against me can prosper! My womb is healthy and strong, full of life and strength. I will be blessed with a healthy baby.

Our infertility journey ends here. My husband's reproductive system works properly, in Jesus' name. My reproductive system is working properly, in Jesus' name. As we read this book, we will be healed and have success in having a healthy baby.

I speak life and healing over my body, my hormones and my uterus. Everything must align with the word of God! I was made to have a baby and carry it full term, and that is what my body will do!

My baby is healthy, no sickness or disease can come against my baby. He/she is made in the perfect image of God. God's hand of protection is over this baby in and out of the womb. I speak life and health into my baby.

I thank You, God, for what a blessing this baby is. Thank You for the great plans You have for his/her life. I thank You that this baby is healthy and strong, that he/she will prosper, and that all he/she does will be successful. Thank You for making me this baby's parent. Help me to love and instruct this baby according to Your word.

God, when trials come my way, help me to trust You. When uncertainty arises, help me to feel Your peace. Give my wisdom for this pregnancy and baby.

Glory and honor to You, God. Thank You for sending angels to protect my baby and me. Thank You that life is forming in my womb. Thank You that as this baby enters the world, he/she will be healthy, full of joy, and strong. I pray that this pregnancy and baby will glorify Your name.

Communion

Communion is a personal, intimate sacrament between the believer and Jesus Christ. It is an outward visible sign of an inward belief and commitment. It represents Christ's body and blood. In the Bible, one of the things the blood represents is protection.

Communion has also been called the meal that heals. Believers take communion to represent what Jesus did on the cross. He died for the forgiveness of our sins, salvation, healing, and deliverance (See Isaiah 53 in the Bible). Christians participate in communion as a means of healing their bodies, as a means of prayer, and as a way to reflect on Jesus' sacrifice and atonement.

There are entire books written on the meaning and importance of the blood of Jesus and partaking in communion. As my editor was working on this book, she was pregnant. She suggested adding a little about the importance of taking communion daily while you are pregnant, and I thought, "What a great idea: taking communion daily as a form of healing and protection for your baby while you are expecting." I could even go a step further and say, if you are infertile and know about the power of communion and how Jesus heals, I would encourage you to take it for your healing.

IS JESUS THE LORD OF YOUR LIFE?

Communion is a sacrament for believers. It means you must have a moment when you stopped, repented of your sins, and asked Jesus to come into your heart and be Lord of your life.

Do you know Jesus, or do you live for Jesus? Have you never committed to Jesus but wonder what it is about? Let me tell you, asking Jesus to come into your heart and take over your life is the best decision you can make. Acknowledging Jesus as Lord is amazing! Living for Him is so wonderful. He will help you through life, make things easier, and you can pray to Him and even hear from Him; He will lead and guide you. But one of the things He does require us to do is turn from our sin, unhealthy habits, negative attitudes, things we know are wrong, and to come and live a life with Jesus and love at the center. Wouldn't you want that for yourself and your baby anyway? If you have never committed your life to Jesus, here is a prayer you can pray aloud now.

PRAYER

Jesus, I repent of my sins. I am sorry for the wrong things I have done. I ask You to forgive me. I forgive myself for the mistakes I have made. I want to live differently, with love, joy, and purpose. I want You to lead and guide me along the way. Today, I decide to live my life for You, and I ask You to come into my heart and be Lord of my life.

Congrats, my friend! The Bible says the angels rejoice when a person comes to the Lord. Now, I want to encourage you to find a friend who goes to church and ask them if you can come with them. If you don't have that option, then turn on the TV or YouTube and find an online church to watch so you can grow in the things of the Lord.

HOW TO TAKE COMMUNION

I realize taking communion may be new for some of you. Perhaps some of you never took it at home without being in a church with a pastor or priest. It's okay! It's easy, and I can walk you through it. You don't need a pastor or priest to bless it. We can bless our own communion and take it at home with Jesus.

You can use a small piece of bread or a cracker. You will also need grape juice. Before taking communion, self-examine and see if there is anything you need to repent of or ask Jesus to forgive you. Meditate and focus on Jesus; maybe listen to a Christian song, sit in silence for a moment, or, if you have been a Christian for a while, pray and talk to Jesus. When you feel your heart is prepared and you have peace, eat the bread which represents His body that was broken for you at the cross, and then drink the juice that represents the blood that was poured out at the cross for your healing, deliverance, and salvation. It only takes a minute or two, unless you want to spend more time with the Lord, which is great!

.

Section 1

Prepping Your Body for Baby

Chapter 1

Stress

We all experience stress, and during pregnancy or while trying to get pregnant, you may experience it too. Managing that stress during this time is important — for your and your baby's health.

Severe stress releases elevated levels of the hormones cortisol and adrenaline. Long-term exposure to these during pregnancy can cause high blood pressure (preeclampsia), increase the risk of preterm birth and low birth weight, and cause gestational diabetes. It can also impact the baby's brain development. Trust God and try to remain peaceful even when things don't go your way. If you aren't pregnant yet, don't stress about not conceiving because stress can hinder you from becoming pregnant.

PRAYER DECLARATIONS

I pray peace over my body and baby.

I command my cortisol and adrenaline levels to be in the normal range.

I say stress, you cannot come near me during this pregnancy.

I rebuke stressful situations, in Jesus' name.

I rebuke stress headaches, muscle tension, overeating, or fatigue caused by stress.

God, I ask for You to show me the joy in this season.

I ask for clarity and vision for this season of life.

I am excited about labor and delivery!

God is my source of strength!

I speak life into my womb!

PRAYER

Father God, I ask for help managing stress during this pregnancy. Help keep my cortisol and adrenaline levels stable and within normal limits. Help my baby not feel any stress that I might undergo while pregnant. Help me to stay at peace in all situations. Help me to handle stress well and remind me that You are my source of peace, God.

SCRIPTURE

Trust in the Lord with all your heart, and lean not on your own understanding.

— Proverbs 3:5

Be anxious for nothing, but in everything, by prayer and supplication with gratitude, make your requests known to God.

— Philippians 4:6

We know that all things work together for good to those who love God, to those who are called according to His purpose.

— Romans 8:28

And the peace of God, which surpasses all understanding, will protect your hearts and minds through Christ Jesus.

— Philippians 4:7

Cast all your care upon Him, because He cares for you.

— 1 Peter 5:7

Chapter 2

Hormones

W e ladies are hormonal. Our hormones rage. We can make light of it, but the truth is, we need balanced hormones for so many areas of our lives. Let's face it, when our hormones are raging, we aren't always the nicest people. In all seriousness, you know your body best. You know what ignites you in a not-so-nice way. Spend time thinking about your personality, perhaps your body changes, what affects your mood, and write some positive prayers to combat those raging feelings. We also want to encourage you to write some declarations for how you need your hormones to align in your body for conception, balance, pregnancy, labor, and milk production.

If you are infertile, praying for your hormones is crucial. There are several declarations about hormones in this book.

PRAYER DECLARATIONS

I pray that my cells accept the right hormones.

I declare that my hormones are balanced perfectly, in Jesus' name.

My body was created to carry children.

I am capable of all that I will endure.

ENDOCRINE SYSTEM

The endocrine system is the body's hormone system. It is responsible for producing and releasing hormones that help regulate growth, metabolism, reproduction, mood, and pregnancy. The endocrine system includes the hypothalamus, pituitary gland, pineal gland, thyroid, parathyroid glands, adrenal glands, pancreas, and ovaries or testes. Other parts of the body also release hormones, including adipose tissue (fat tissue), the kidneys, the liver, the gut, and the placenta.

PRAYER DECLARATIONS

I speak to my fat tissue, kidneys, liver, gut, and placenta and say you will release hormones properly and function the way God designed you to.

I command communication through my endocrine system to work properly.

I command communication between my endocrine system and my organs to function properly.

HUMAN CHORIONIC GONADOTROPIN (HCG)

Human chorionic gonadotropin is a hormone made during pregnancy, primarily by the placenta. It helps support the pregnancy in the early stages and is often associated with nausea and vomiting.

PRAYER DECLARATIONS

I pray for human chorionic gonadotropin to rise in early pregnancy to help my body maintain this pregnancy. I pray it does not cause nausea or vomiting, in Jesus' name.

I command that the placenta will produce the proper amount of hCG that my body and baby need.

PROGESTERONE

Progesterone supports pregnancy by maintaining the uterine lining and helping the body sustain pregnancy. Changes in progesterone levels can also contribute to fatigue and mood changes.

PRAYER DECLARATIONS

I pray over my progesterone levels and command them to work properly during pregnancy, in Jesus' name.

I speak to my progesterone levels and say you will help increase and maintain the uterine lining needed to carry this pregnancy.

I rebuke excessive mood swings, fatigue, and miscarriage, in Jesus' name.

ESTROGEN

Estrogen increases during pregnancy and supports the baby's development, breast milk supply and overall pregnancy health.

PRAYER DECLARATIONS

Estrogen levels will rise during this pregnancy, in Jesus' name.

Estrogen will help my breasts develop and prepare to produce milk to feed my baby.

Body, you will produce the correct amount of estrogen to help maintain a healthy pregnancy.

MID-PREGNANCY (SECOND TRIMESTER)

During the second trimester, the placenta begins producing most of the progesterone and estrogen, gradually replacing the role of the ovaries.

PRAYER DECLARATION

Placenta, I speak to you and say you will produce progesterone and estrogen to maintain a healthy pregnancy.

HUMAN PLACENTAL LACTOGEN (HPL)

Human placental lactogen is a hormone produced by the placenta. It supports the baby's nutrition, helps regulate the mother's blood sugar levels, and prepares the breasts for breastfeeding.

PRAYER DECLARATIONS

Placenta, I pray that you produce human placental lactogen. It will regulate my glucose levels and prepare my breasts for breastfeeding.

I command that my baby receives proper nutrition from the placenta.

PROLACTIN

Prolactin levels rise during pregnancy to prepare the body for milk production.

PRAYER DECLARATION

I speak to prolactin and command it to increase and prepare my body for breastfeeding.

LATE PREGNANCY (THIRD TRIMESTER)

During the third trimester, progesterone and estrogen reach peak levels to help prepare the body for labor and breastfeeding.

PRAYER DECLARATIONS

As I enter the third trimester, I pray that my progesterone and estrogen levels reach their peak and prepare my body for labor and breastfeeding.

I declare that human placental lactogen continues to nourish my baby and support healthy milk gland development.

As my body and baby are ready for delivery, I pray that hormone levels shift appropriately to allow labor to begin naturally.

HORMONE DISRUPTORS

Some chemicals can disrupt the body's natural hormonal balance, interfering with the endocrine system. We strongly encourage you to try and minimize these from your life, not just during pregnancy but forever, as they will disrupt your hormones for your lifetime.

Examples include:

- BPA, found in plastics, store receipts, some canned foods, and epoxy linings
- Phthalates, used in plastics, food packaging, and cosmetics
- Dioxins, found in industrial byproducts and contaminated foods
- Certain pesticides, such as atrazine
- Flame retardants, including PBDEs and PFAS
- Triclosan, used in soaps and personal care products
- Phytoestrogens, which can mimic estrogen and are commonly found in soy

PRAYER DECLARATION

I choose wisely what I expose my body to, and I trust God to help my body regulate hormones as He designed it to. I command all side effects or deposits of harmful chemicals into my bloodstream to leave me now, in Jesus' name.

Chapter 3

Birth Control

Reverse Side Effects

irth control appears to be a common logical solution to not having children. I am not saying you are wrong, but we haven't been educated about the possible outcomes of what appears to be an easy solution. Birth control basically tells your body not to ovulate. The result is that it messes with your hormones and your body's natural rhythm. When you stop taking it, some women's bodies will return to normal, but in the case of others, their bodies aren't returning to the way God designed. Side effects can include weight gain and mental effects. However, the ultimate price some women will pay is that they will not be able to get pregnant or will struggle getting pregnant for years because the pill shuts their bodies down for so long that they are no longer responding.

We want to say there is no condemnation. I, (Kathy), was on birth control for years. I know the frustration of not being able to get pregnant.

We tried for over a year before we conceived. I didn't know the side effects. I don't condemn myself, and you shouldn't condemn yourself either. The Bible says, *"There is therefore now no condemnation for those who are in Christ Jesus, who walk not according to the flesh, but according to the Spirit"* (Romans 8:1).

Let the past go and believe that your body will come back into alignment with these prayers. Healing is available here and now!

PRAYER

God, I ask You to meet me here and now to heal my body of any negative side effects birth control has had on me. I am sorry for what I did or didn't know, and I ask Your forgiveness if I did anything wrong. I also forgive myself if I am holding myself responsible. I am redeemed and healed. My body and hormones are coming back into alignment with how You created me. I cast out any negative side effects and claim healing, in Jesus' name. I thank You, Lord, that my body will ovulate and produce the perfect number of children You have planned for my life.

PRAYER DECLARATIONS

I renounce any negative side effects from birth control, and I say they will stop, in Jesus' name.

If any weight gain or mood changes are caused by birth control, I pray that you will go now, in Jesus' name.

Hormones, I order you to balance back out.

My hormones will all come into alignment with the word of God.

I pray over my ovaries and uterus, and I command them to work properly as God created them to, in Jesus' name.

I speak life into my uterus and ovaries.

I pray my cycle returns to regular rotation.

I speak and claim my body will ovulate optimally.

Ovulation will occur monthly and be pain and cramp-free.

My progesterone levels will return to normal.

The uterine lining will be restored and healthy.

Vaginal discharge comes forth at normal levels.

ALTERNATIVE METHODS TO BIRTH CONTROL PILL

If you are trying to heal your hormones or stay away from harsh chemicals, do your research and find clean or healthier versions of condoms.

Natural Family Planning is a popular, natural option. You track your cycle to know when you are ovulating versus when you are not. Books can teach you how to use this method. In addition to this method, you can use ovulation test strips, which work like a pregnancy test. You can tell whether you are ovulating by using the test strips correctly.

Chapter 4

Uterine and Cervical Prayers

For You have formed my inward parts; You have covered me in my mother's womb.

— Psalm 139:13

PRAYER DECLARATIONS

My uterus is of normal shape and size and is not distorted or formed into ways that could prevent pregnancy and delivery.

My cervix is normal in size and shape. Sperm can get through my cervix with ease and enter the uterus to fertilize an egg!

My organs produce the proper amount of cervical mucus for great implantation. I am going to have a baby!

God made all my parts perfect and complete! My female organs are in great shape to conceive and sustain pregnancy.

I command t-cells to destroy any cancer that is attempting to manifest in my body.

I command all cancerous and non-cancerous growths to dissolve in the name of Jesus.

Fibroid tumors, in the name of Jesus, you will disappear.

My body does not produce uterine polyps. Any existing polyps must dissipate, in Jesus' name.

I will not have noncancerous growths that can distort the uterine cavity, making implantation difficult.

Chapter 5

Conception — Let's Start
Trying!

Prayers and declarations to command your body into perfect alignment so that conception, implantation, and the baby comes forth! Begin to believe you will receive! Get all doubt and unbelief out. If you have tried before and it didn't work out as you planned, know that now you have a different battle plan and medically specific prayers. Let us be your cheerleaders, root for you, and pray for you!

Submit a prayer request at kathydegrawministries.org!

PRAYER DECLARATIONS

My brain, specifically the hypothalamus, speaks to my body and sends signals to initiate a menstrual cycle.

My pituitary gland functions normally and releases key hormones needed for conception, ovulation and pregnancy.

My follicle-stimulating hormone works properly, stimulating the ovaries to grow follicles that contain immature eggs. My eggs are abundant, strong, and healthy.

My body produces estrogen to thicken the uterine lining in preparation for a fertilized egg.

My fallopian tubes are lined with healthy cilia to carry the egg and sperm. There are no blockages or obstacles in my fallopian tubes.

Cervical mucus is changing to help the sperm survive and reach my egg.

I call forth my luteinizing hormone to trigger ovulation and the release of a mature egg. My eggs are not deformed; they are fully grown, developed, and viable. My eggs are fertilizable.

I claim my mature egg comes out of the follicle and into the fallopian tube.

My egg will be fertilized!

I order my uterine lining to thicken to 7-12mm for implantation, be well nourished, and be blood-rich. My embryo will plant securely into the uterine wall.

Upon conception, my body produces progesterone, which keeps the uterine lining thick and stable. It will hold the embryo in place, and the egg will form a baby. The egg will plant both deeply and securely.

The hormone hCG signals my body to continue producing progesterone. I will maintain a healthy, full-term pregnancy.

I command that after conception, my cervix stay closed for a full-term pregnancy.

My ovaries produce the hormones necessary for conception, fetal development, and the baby's health.

Section 2

Fertility

Chapter 6

Fertilization

Y ou got this, girlfriend! Open your mouth, lay hands on your abdomen, anoint yourself with holy anointing prayer oil, and speak out these declarations, loudly and authoritatively! Call forth life! The power comes in praying these prayers audibly. You need to SPEAK OUT to SPEAK LIFE! Pray these prayers aloud in a passionate, authoritative voice, and command your body to align with God's will for your life.

Waiting for a child causes great internal pain and struggle, as we learn from Hannah.

But to Hannah, he gave a double portion because he loved Hannah, but the LORD had closed her womb. Now her rival provoked her greatly, making her miserable because the LORD had closed her womb. Thus it was yearly, when she went up to the house of the LORD, that she provoked her. So Hannah wept and did not eat. Then said Elkanah her husband to her, "Hannah, why are you weeping? And why do you not eat? Why is your heart grieved? Am I not better to you than ten sons?" So Hannah arose after they had eaten in Shiloh and after they had drunk. Now Eli the priest was sitting on a seat by the door of the tabernacle of the LORD. And she was bitter, and prayed to the LORD, and wept severely. So she made a vow and said, "O LORD of Hosts, if You will indeed look on the affliction of Your maidservant, and remember me and not forget Your maidservant, but will give to Your maidservant a baby boy, then I will give him to the LORD all the days of his life, and no razor shall touch his head." And as she was praying before the LORD, Eli watched her mouth. Now Hannah was speaking in her heart. Her lips were moving, but her voice was not heard. Therefore, Eli thought she was drunk. So Eli said to her, "How long will you be drunk? Put away your wine from you." And Hannah answered and said, "No, my Lord, I am a woman of sorrow. I have drunk neither wine nor strong drink, but have poured out my soul before the LORD. Do not consider your handmaid to be a sinful woman, for out of the abundance of my concern and provocation I have spoken until now." Then Eli answered and said, "Go in peace, and the God of Israel grant you your request that you have asked of Him." And she said, "Let your handmaid find grace in your sight." So the woman went her way and ate, and her face was not sad as before. They rose up in the morning early and worshipped before the LORD. And they returned and came to their house to Ramah. And Elkanah knew Hannah his wife, and the LORD remembered her. And it came to pass that Hannah conceived and bore a son. And she called his name Samuel saying, "Because I have asked him of the LORD."

— 1 Samuel 1:5-20

Hannah was sad. Elkanah, her husband, was trying to make her feel better by saying, "Aren't I better than 10 sons?" Let's be honest. We love our spouses, but when we yearn for a child, it is hard. The emptiness and loneliness we feel. Nothing can replace the loss of desiring a child of your own. Find a trusted, faith-filled friend who is a faith giant, and talk to them. Have them pray with you and encourage you. Surround yourself with people who will lift you, believe with you, and believe for you!

I want you to note what Hannah did next in her anguish: she prayed. She may not have felt like praying, but she did. I remember when something devastating happened in my ministry. I wanted to quit and give up. However, with tears streaming down my face, mad, angry, treated unfairly, and grieving, I turned to the Lord, and I worshipped and prayed. I was in so much pain, yet I prayed and worshipped. No matter where you are, you need to believe that God will hear your prayers, but you need to keep praying even when you aren't seeing the manifestation of your prayers. My story ended up several times better because of what happened.

Hannah poured out her soul before the Lord. One thing I have discovered is that people don't pray; they expect God to do it, whether it is a baby or something else they want. They sit back and don't understand why they don't have it, when the truth is, they aren't praying for it. Once she heard the Lord was going to answer her prayer, she worshipped. I want to encourage you: when the Lord answers your prayers, worship, testify of his goodness, give a love offering to the Lord, and go out and celebrate His goodness. I love celebrating the goodness of the Lord. When He does something extraordinary, I go out to dinner, give a financial donation to a ministry, or somehow celebrate what He has done. Some people go in faith and do something like that as a seed or positive declaration in expectation of what He will do.

PRAYER DECLARATIONS

I order my brain to release follicle-stimulating and luteinizing hormones. My hypothalamus signals the pituitary glands to release these hormones, preparing for ovulation.

I instruct my follicle-stimulating hormone to stimulate the growth of follicles to contain immature eggs.

My follicles grow and release estrogen, thickening the uterine lining to prepare for implantation.

My LH triggers ovulation with a mature follicle to release an egg into the fallopian tube.

I take authority over the egg that releases and say that you will remain viable and be fertilized, in the name of Jesus, who produces and sustains life.

I order the sperm to be present in the fallopian tube at the time of ovulation.

I say and proclaim that the sperm are strong swimmers and reach their destination.

My husband produces the proper amount of strong and healthy sperm. He does not have a low sperm count but has more than enough to fertilize an egg.

My husband's sperm does not die off prematurely. They are survivors.

The sperm in my uterus stay in the reproductive tract, alive and healthy, for the proper length of days that God has designed.

The sperm in my uterus stay alive and increase my fertility window.

Sperm, I instruct you to meet and fertilize my eggs.

The sperm deposited into me penetrates the outer layer of the egg and fuses with it, creating a fertilized egg.

My husband's sperm cell penetrates my egg, creating life.

The zygote begins to divide, becoming a blastocyst, as it moves uninterrupted through the fallopian tube toward the uterus.

The cells are healthy and strong as they divide.

I command my uterine lining to be thick.

My uterine wall is nutrient-rich and receptive to receiving the blastocyst (embryo).

The blastocyst (embryo) implants properly into my uterine wall.

I direct my uterus to grow and expand to receive the embryo.

The embryo attaches and grows properly in my uterine wall.

I decree hCG signals the corpus luteum to produce progesterone, supporting the uterine lining and preventing menstruation.

I order the placenta to begin forming and to nourish a healthy, strong, developing embryo.

Chapter 7

Healthy and Abundant Eggs

I t is important to take authority over all things. We are praying specifically for everything that needs to happen to help you get pregnant and set you up for success! Believe that if God did it for Sarah in the Bible, He will do it for you too!

Children are a heritage from the LORD, offspring a reward from him. Like arrows in the hands of a warrior are children born in one's youth.

— Psalm 127:3-5

PRAYER DECLARATIONS

I rebuke and cancel the medical statistics that claim my quality and quantity of eggs diminish after 35 years of age. I defy the odds and normal statistics.

My age does not matter. As Sarah conceived in her old age (Genesis 21:1-7), I, too, can conceive past 35.

"One of them said, *'I will certainly return to you about this time next year, and Sarah your wife will have a son.' And Sarah heard it in the tent door, which was behind him"* (Genesis 18:10).

I speak and decree that I am not under a curse and that I shall bear children. *"God blessed them and said to them, 'Be fruitful and multiply, and fill the earth and subdue it'"* (Genesis 1:28).

I bind and restrict early menopause and declare that my ovaries will function normally.

I do not and will not have premature ovarian insufficiency. I will be fruitful and multiply.

I rebuke the curse that age is against me for fertilization and a healthy pregnancy.

I have an abundant supply of eggs, and they release correctly. They respond to the words of declaration that I speak over my body.

I am positive that I have a substantial ovarian reserve. I will not stress or fear about my biological clock ticking away the ability to conceive.

I will not worry about my age, but will have perfect peace that God's timing for fertilization and children is in His plan and will for my life.

Chapter 8

Endometriosis

I have witnessed God heal women of endometriosis. I want you to know I have been healed of 17 different issues in my life. We serve a healing God. It is one of the reasons Jesus died on the cross to purchase your healing. I know doctors have told you, "You can't," "It will be hard," or "You have this condition." Doctors don't have the final say, Jesus does! I have been in a healing ministry for years and have seen God do what doctors said can't be done. One component of healing is raising your faith to align with the word of God. If you don't have faith to be healed and need prayer, send for a prayer cloth, and we will anoint it and pray over you. We have had testimonies of people being healed using these cloths. Prayer cloths are mentioned in Acts 19:11-12.

Get your mind in a good place. Believe God for the impossible. If you need help receiving healing in your body, I have written a book titled *Healed at Last*. It is more than a book; it is a guidebook to help you walk through healing. It will increase your faith! If you don't believe me, read over 100 reviews on Amazon on how a person's life was changed by reading the book.

PRAYER DECLARATIONS

I curse endometriosis in my body. I command any tissue growing outside the uterus wall that is damaging my body to cease to exist, in Jesus' name.

Any existing tissue, I tell you to stop attaching to the ovaries, fallopian tubes, the outer surfaces of the uterus, the bladder, the intestines, and other pelvic organs.

I command my body to stop the progression and effects of endometriosis in my body. I order all abnormal tissue growth to come to a halt in the name of Jesus.

I thwart the formation of scar tissue and adhesions in the name of Jesus.

I command that I will not have any chronic inflammation or damage to the ovaries, fallopian tubes, and uterus.

All scar tissue, I order you to dissolve. You will not block the fallopian tubes, preventing the egg and sperm from meeting.

I proclaim my immune system is in perfect working order. Any abnormal immune system responses are healed now in the mighty name of Jesus. You will not attack sperm or embryos or make implantation difficult.

I have a healthy hormone environment. No inflammation or abnormal tissue growth is affecting my hormones, causing problems with ovulation, egg release, or uterine lining receptivity.

Chapter 9

Fallopian Tubes

Nothing is impossible for God (Luke 1:37). I, (Kathy), have prayed for several women who had blocked fallopian tubes or challenges getting pregnant, and God healed them. If you have been told you have a fallopian tube issue, believe Jesus as Healer. Command blockages to be gone or pray for the blood of Jesus to flow through your tubes, order the fire of God to burn up any blockages. It doesn't matter what you pray, but that you do pray. Expect God to do the impossible so you can be a testimony to your doctor and so that the name of Jesus can be glorified and lifted high.

PRAYER DECLARATIONS

I command any spirit of infirmity and infection in my fallopian tubes to be removed now, in Jesus' name. I declare I am healed.

I call forth properly working, fully attached and developed fallopian tubes. I say I do not have any congenital problems in my fallopian tubes.

I decree there are no adverse reactions or lasting effects from prior surgeries causing damage to my fallopian tubes and the surrounding areas.

I command any damage from pelvic inflammatory disease, STDs, or endometriosis to be reversed and dissipate in the matchless name of Jesus. I repent for any STD and anything that I participated in to open the door to sickness in my body.

I speak to any fibroids, tumors and cysts, in and around the uterus and fallopian tubes. I order you to destroy yourselves and dissolve in the name of Jesus.

I command scar tissue to dissolve, in Jesus' name. Scar tissue, I speak to you, I command you to dissipate, dissolve and disappear in the name of Jesus. Body be healed, in Jesus' name.

I take the authority and dominion Jesus gave me and order any obstruction, thickening, or defect to dissipate and burn up by the fire of God.

I call forth that my fallopian tubes are open and that sperm and eggs can move freely through my tubes. There is no narrowing of my tubes from STDs, previous injuries, surgery, or deformation.

Jesus, You gave me power and authority over all things; therefore, I take authority over my fallopian tubes and instruct you to work properly.

I restrict ectopic pregnancies. I say the fertilized egg will plant properly in the uterine lining. I bind and restrict ectopic pregnancies and death from coming upon my child and me. I will have a viable, full-term pregnancy!

I call forth creative miracles in my reproductive parts and any part that is missing or malfunctioning. I tell you to be healed, and if not present, appear and come forth, in Jesus' name.

I thank You, Lord, that You said be fruitful and multiply, (Genesis 9:1), and that You desire to give me children, (Psalm 127:3).

> *God blessed them and said to them, 'Be fruitful and multiply, and fill the earth and subdue it. Rule over the fish of the sea and over the birds of the air and over every living thing that moves on the earth.*
>
> — Genesis 1:28

Section 3

Infertility / IVF

Chapter 10

Infertility

Then Esau looked up and saw the women and children. 'Who are these with you?' he asked. Jacob answered, 'They are the children God has graciously given your servant.'

— Genesis 33:5

For this child I prayed, and the Lord has granted me my petition which I asked of Him.

— 1 Samuel 1:27

I haven't been where you are, but I have been in a similar place. I never want to say I know what you are feeling, because two people can be going through infertility, but how it affects each of them is individual and personal. I, (Kathy), did experience the pain of infertility for a year—the pain of my sister and sister-in-law both being pregnant at the same time, our closest friend group with babies and pregnancies, and the pain of not being able to walk down the baby food aisle at the grocery store without crying.

Even so, I want to validate that your feelings are real and that the pain is raw. Although I have walked a similar path, I am not in your shoes.

BELIEVE AND DECLARE

There will be no miscarriages or infertility in your land, and I will give you long, full lives.

— Exodus 23:26

Women were barren in the Bible. The barren women gave birth to a child in every case except one. When we discover barrenness in the Bible, it is often connected to destiny and a great call of God on the child's life. Therefore, there is a spiritual issue we need to pray against called spiritual warfare. Spiritual warfare occurs when God wants something to happen in the natural, but unseen forces or circumstances prevent it from manifesting. When warfare arises, it doesn't necessarily mean one of the parents has a physical condition preventing conception, but it is warfare against the child. Precise prayers must be sent forth to dispel the attacks of warfare.

When we look biblically, all the children born of barrenness had great purpose, such as Isaac, Joseph, Samson, Samuel, Jacob, and John the Baptist. When we look at how they conceived and what happened to bring them to bear children, we learn that prayer, visitation, and God's grace were upon these women. Prayer moved God's heart as Isaac prayed for Rebekah, and Hannah poured out her soul before the Lord. It is one of the reasons we created this book: to help you pray your baby forth into destiny. God wants us to pray. There is only one case in the entire Bible in which a barren woman did not conceive. I like those statistics, and I pray that they give you hope that sometimes our children coming forth is in God's timing. We do see this in the case of these barren women. I don't like to say they were barren because they did conceive; it was simply delayed.

We see in Scripture that the delay was due to prophetic timing, the fulfillment of promises, or to God's glory being revealed by knowing that He alone could make this happen. Unfortunately, the delay in our destiny and our children does not make waiting easier. It is difficult when you long in your heart to hold a baby. The hurt, pain, tears, and grief that you've yet to experience are real and raw. Our God is sovereign, and He knows so many things that we do not, and that is where we have to try to find peace, hope, and patience to wait upon His timing. I know there have been several instances where I said I needed to go through this before this could happen. He sees things we don't. I also think we should look at the stories of the Bible. If we are really sold out to God and our child has a big destiny like the babies who were produced out of barrenness had, if God showed us that in advance, would we be a little more willing to wait?

Another factor that is often overlooked when discussing delayed conception is spiritual opposition. I believe this played a role in my own experience. After a year of infertility, my son was born under distress and had to be resuscitated twice. Years later, as a child, he began praying that God would use him in a healing ministry.

Scripture shows a consistent pattern of the enemy attempting to hinder firstborn sons when there is a strong calling attached to their lives. Looking back, I believe there was a spiritual battle surrounding my womb and my child's destiny.

FROM BARRENNESS TO BIRTHING DESTINY

I want you to have hope, so let's dive into Scripture and study how these women overcame to have a child!

SARAH

Sarah and Abraham were married. Sarah grew impatient at not being able to bear a child and gave her servant, Hagar, to her husband so that Hagar could conceive. She took things into her own hands because she wasn't having a child in her timing. Pray. Use caution and discernment. Seek the Holy Spirit. Ask Him about His timing and His plan for children.

I admire my daughter Lauren; she always sought the Lord and left her children in His hands and timing.

Adoption is a beautiful option, and there is also IVF as an alternative, and for some, surrogacy, but stop and pray before taking an alternative option. Ask the Spirit of the Lord for His will for your life. If you decide to take one of these routes, pray and ask for His permission and blessing. Don't run ahead of what the Lord has planned for you.

Sarah was barren into her old age when medical science would say it was impossible. God visited her and gave her a son, Isaac. Keep believing and put more faith in your God than in the doctors.

God visited Sarah. He divinely intervened. The word visited means to intervene, to perform, to activate destiny. God intervened to activate the promise. However, before the intervention, He changed Sarai's identity before opening her womb, including changing her name to Sarah. When we study Scripture, we see that God changed Sarah's name, decreed that she would be a mother to nations, and blessed her. Ask yourself, or pray and seek the Holy Spirit, if there is anything that needs to change in your life before you can become a mom. I'm not saying there is, but I always like to self-evaluate and see if God wants to reveal anything.

REBEKAH

Rebekah was barren for years and was married to Isaac. Now, note that this was the same Isaac who had just been born to Sarah, who could not conceive. The Bible does not state that this is a generational curse. However, as I have been a deliverance minister for years, I would definitely suggest praying off and breaking any generational curses to barrenness if you or your husband's parents had the same issue.

As we look at Rebekah, we see that Isaac prayed for her to conceive. I realize some husbands are not active in praying for the women and standing in spiritual agreement. Still, I encourage you, women, to try to get your husband on the same page, because it was as Isaac prayed that the conception happened. We put specific prayers in this book for your husband. Prayers for your conception, baby, and pregnancy, and prayers for him if he has any male fertility issues.

Sit down together, pray, and call forth your children. It may be awkward, but you can start by joining together to read the prayers from this book. I would suggest getting another copy of the book so you both have in your own places, and then, when you come together, you could repeat the prayers together.

RACHEL

Rachel was one of Jacob's wives, but one he loved most deeply. She was jealous of her sister Leah, who was having several children. It can be difficult emotionally when your friends and siblings are having children, and you aren't. I remember when I was trying to get pregnant with my first, and my sister and sister-in-law were both pregnant. It was difficult, not only did I want a baby, but I thought it would be great for all of us to be pregnant and have children the same age.

Rachel longed so much for children, she said, "Give me children, or else I die" (Genesis 30:1). Jacob responded with only God can give children (Genesis 30:2). I think that is important to remember, whether natural, adoptive, or IVF, God is still the giver of life. It is in His timing. We can do things in the natural, but truly, there is nothing we can do about it. We are surrendered to the Lord and His plan for our lives.

God does care about Rachel. He listened to and opened her womb and gave her children. He did not forget about her, and He didn't forget about you. He cares for you and your offspring. I believe a lot of the time, we delay our own pregnancy because we are striving so hard to conceive. We stress ourselves out with negative pregnancy tests and not becoming pregnant, so stress is the real factor and contributor to our not having a baby.

MANOAH'S WIFE

There was a certain man from Zorah, from the tribe of Dan. His name was Manoah. His wife was infertile and had borne no children. The angel of the LORD appeared to the woman and said to her, "Indeed, you are infertile and have borne no children, yet you will conceive and bear a son. Now be careful, I pray, that you drink no wine or strong drink and that you do not eat anything ritually unclean. For you will conceive and bear a son. No razor may touch his head, for the boy will be a Nazirite to God from the womb. He will begin to save Israel from the hand of the Philistine." (Judges 13:2-5)

This woman miraculously conceived after an angelic visitation. She probably wasn't expecting it, but was open to it. Don't close your heart in the process of waiting. You never know when God will turn your situation around. Therefore, "Pray without ceasing," (1 Thessalonians 5:16). I hear it often, "I am mad at God," or people blaming God, even though we know He is sovereign enough to make it happen. Try not to go to a negative emotional place or get angry at God because it is not happening. Trust Him with the wisdom of His perfect plan.

I like how the angel gave her instructions. I think this is something you could pray into if you are infertile. Ask the Holy Spirit. Are there instructions, something I need to be doing, or anything I need to change in my life or diet? Pray further and ask the Holy Spirit if there are spiritual or natural blockages you need to tear down in prayer. He knows everything. Speak to Him and expect an answer about your situation. Pray over several weeks, not daily, but revisit those questions as you feel the unction, so you can see if there is a roadblock or something else you need to do.

ELIZABETH

There was in the days of Herod, the king of Judea, a certain priest named Zechariah, of the division of Abijah. And his wife was of the daughters of Aaron, and her name was Elizabeth. They were both righteous before God, walking in all the commandments and ordinances of the Lord blamelessly. But they had no child, because Elizabeth was barren, and they both were now well advanced in years. Now while he served as priest before God, when his division was on duty, according to the custom of the priest's office, his lot was to burn incense when he went into the temple of the Lord. And the whole crowd of people were praying outside at the hour of incense. Then an angel of the Lord appeared to him, standing on the right side of the altar of incense. When Zechariah saw him, he was troubled, and fear fell upon him. But the angel said to him, "Do not fear, Zechariah, for your prayer has been heard, and your wife Elizabeth will bear you a son, and you shall call his name John. You will have joy and gladness, and many will rejoice at his birth. For he will be great in the sight of the Lord, and shall drink neither wine nor strong drink, and he will be filled with the Holy Spirit, even from his mother's womb. He will turn many of the sons of Israel to the Lord their God."

— Luke 1:5-16

The first thing I want you to see is that they were both walking right with the Lord and obeying His commands, yet they were barren. Often, we don't know why the Lord delays, but know this: you did nothing wrong to deserve barrenness; God is not mad at you or punishing you. They were doing everything right and were barren. We live in a fallen world, and sometimes it just doesn't make sense, but we are called to walk in trust and faith. Don't blame yourself or your spouse.

She was aged and barren, yet God enabled her to conceive John the Baptist. God is ultimately in control. You have to breathe, trust, and pray. He gave her a child against all odds, and no matter what medical professionals have told you or diagnosed you with, God can turn it around. Surround yourself with strong Christian believers who will be your cheerleaders and lift you. Focus on living in the moment and not worrying about the future.

WHAT WE LEARN FROM BIBLICAL BARRENNESS

- God can close the womb (Genesis 20:18).
- God is the one who opens the womb (Genesis 29:31).
- Prayer opens the womb and changes the outcome.
- It isn't always medical procedures that help us conceive.

- Divine intervention can open the womb.
- Barrenness was not always physical.
- Delay is not denial.
- Birthing children is part of a prophetic timeline and a release of destiny.
- Spiritual warfare over the womb and the promise of God is real.
- The enemy will always fight the generational line.
- Delay does not mean God has abandoned you.
- Spiritual destiny often attracts resistance.
- Pray into God's promise, His word, and His plans for your life.
- Timing is sometimes involved. God spoke (Genesis 18:14), *"At the appointed time…Sarah shall have a son."*

While writing this book, the Lord gave me greater compassion for parents and grandparents who aren't living their dream of having a child. Please know that we are praying this book helps you birth the dreams and desires of your heart.

PRAYER DECLARATIONS

My brain works properly. I command the hypothalamus to regulate my hormones and maintain regular ovulation.

My hormones are perfectly balanced as God designed me in my mother's womb. My hormones will help produce life.

My thyroid performs optimally. It is not overactive or underactive. I order my thyroid not to disrupt the menstrual cycle and fertility. I will be fertile!

I forbid ovarian insufficiency. I will have normal ovarian functions and produce a regular supply of eggs for as long as I need to create the number of children I want, no matter what my age.

I bind and rebuke polycystic ovary syndrome. I will not have hormonal disorders causing irregular periods, cysts on the ovaries, or infrequent ovulation.

I call forth regular, consistent ovulation cycles.

I disrupt any attempt of a bacterial infection to cause damage to my reproductive organs and fallopian tubes. I am redeemed from every spirit of infirmity (Galatians 3:13).

I command any and all fibroids and polyps to disappear. I order you to leave my body now, in Jesus' name. Fire of God, burn up any growths in my body!

I speak to my cervix and cervical mucus. I proclaim my mucus is normal and the opening of my cervix is adequate for sperm to enter the uterus.

I decree my periods will not be irregular or absent. My body will remain fertile, and every function will work properly for exactly the number of years I need to carry multiple children.

Chapter 11

Polycystic Ovary Syndrome (PCOS)

PCOS is a hormone disorder in women. It commonly causes hormonal imbalances and irregular periods, which can lead to ovarian cysts. It is a common issue, with one in ten women of childbearing age dealing with it. It is one of the primary causes of infertility. But it doesn't just affect you during your childbearing years—it affects you your whole life.

If PCOS is what doctors have diagnosed you with, the good news is that our God is a healer and a miracle-working God. Medically, you can still get pregnant; it just might take a little longer. According to medical research, people with PCOS often have more eggs, which means their childbearing window can be longer.

In Genesis 21, we find the story of Sarah. Sarah wanted so badly to have children, but was never able to conceive. Yet at 90, God fulfilled her heart's desire. *"For Sarah conceived and bore Abraham a son in his old age, at the set time that God had spoken to him,* (Genesis 21:2).

We are not medical doctors, but from what I have observed, PCOS is enhanced by obesity and diabetes. When we want the Lord to heal us, we also need to do our part in the natural. So, if you are struggling with either of these conditions, I encourage you to pray and ask the Holy Spirit for the strength and wisdom to overcome them. Do your part in the natural by moving, drinking water, reducing sugar and gluten, and doing what you know needs to be done. You can't always do it for yourself, but do it for your spouse and your future kids. Arise! You can do it! If your PCOS is highly hormone-related, see the section on hormones for prayers and how you can remove hormone disrupters from your life.

PRAYER

We speak life, health, and healing into your body. PCOS cannot persist in your body. You are healed and made whole. Your periods are regular. Your insulin levels are normal. Your testosterone levels are normal.

PRAYER DECLARATIONS

I speak to my hormones and command them to come into alignment with the word of God.

I say my testosterone levels are normal, and I say my ovaries produce the proper amount of testosterone, in Jesus' name.

I speak to my adrenal glands and command them to work properly.

I speak to my body and command it to process insulin correctly.

I decree my body will process and absorb carbohydrates, sugars and proteins well.

I speak to the cysts on my ovaries and command them to break down and disintegrate.

I command all cysts to leave my ovaries now in the name of Jesus.

I declare my periods are regular and consistent.

I call forth creative miracles in my body and proclaim that my ovaries are healthy and function normally.

I am healed of PCOS! I can conceive, and my body aligns with the word of God. I will have children!

I claim and believe getting pregnant will be easy for me.

I rebuke any negative doctor reports concerning this diagnosis, in Jesus' name.

I rebuke medical reports and statistics that say this will affect me for the rest of my life. I do not believe and receive that report and claim that by Jesus' stripes I am healed and made whole.

Chapter 12

IVF Implantation

Joseph said to his father, "They are my sons whom God has given me here."

— Genesis 48:9

He gives the barren woman a home and makes her the joyful mother of children.

— Psalm 113:9

If you are in this position, we are sorry. We know it must not be easy. We can't pretend to understand what you are going through. We merely want you to know we care about you and are praying for a successful journey.

PRAYER DECLARATIONS

My body will respond to the medications needed for IVF. There will be no poor response. My body receives, and I believe! I have trust in the Lord!

I will have successful ovarian stimulation. I declare and believe that I will have enough mature eggs produced, and I will not fear insufficiency.

I call my body to perfect order. I will not have too many follicles. There will be no swelling or fluid issues.

The sperm are of superior performance.

My eggs will be of excellent quality and successfully retrieved. There will be no harm to my eggs in the medical facility.

I plead the blood of Jesus on my eggs. No eggs will be damaged during retrieval.

I call for successful fertilization in the lab. Give the technician the skill and wisdom to make the connection.

I constrain more than one sperm from entering an egg. There will be no abnormal fertilization happening.

Upon fertilization, I expect the embryo to grow strongly and reach the blastocyst stage. There will be no delay or defect.

I praise you in advance, Jesus, that my embryos will develop and reach the blastocyst stage.

I have high quality embryos! There are no genetic defects or slow growth because God, my Father, makes everything perfect and cares about my children.

I call forth my uterine lining to grow to an ideal thickness of 7-12mm.

I command my uterine lining to be receptive. It is not and will not be too thin, inflamed, or not hormonally acceptable.

I will have a gentle and precise embryo transfer. I pray for protection over the transfer. No tool will damage anything during the procedure. The technician will operate with precision.

There will be no trauma caused to the uterine lining during transfer. The embryo plants in the uterus without difficulty, stays where it belongs, and grows into a healthy baby.

I order my body to come into alignment with natural pregnancy and proper hormonal support after the transfer. I say my body will kick in and do what it was designed to do.

The embryo will plant perfectly into the uterus. There will be no misalignment, in Jesus' name. The embryo will grow into a full-term pregnancy with no miscarriage.

My age has nothing to do with my baby implanting and staying healthy. If Sarah in the Bible had a baby at 90, I can have a baby at my age.

I bind and rebuke a spirit of death against my child(ren).

I abort any attempt of the enemy to steal the opportunity of me having children.

I thank You, Lord, that it is Your desire that I have children. I don't have to worry about failed fertilization because I am in Your hands. Eggs, I say you will be fertilized, grow and develop.

Section 4

Male Infertility and Pregnancy Prayers

Chapter 13

Male Infertility Prayers

In Genesis 5, the entire chapter is about how multiple men of God began having children after age 65. I realize people lived much longer in biblical times. Here's the thing, though, you're not alone. If you feel like you're too old to have kids or you have been trying for a long time, God hears your prayers. Sarah was 90 years old before God answered her prayers.

Here are some male reproductive prayers. I have written these for women to pray, since this is a book for women, but men, I highly encourage you to turn them around and speak them aloud over yourself. Please partner with your wife and pray these prayers audibly over yourself!

PRAYER DECLARATIONS

My husband's pituitary gland works properly. There is no malfunction in his brain's hormone center to interfere with sperm production. His pituitary gland secretes the hormones needed for sperm production.

My husband's hormones are in proper chemical balance. His testosterone is at normal levels. He does not have low fluctuations of testosterone. He has adequate sperm production and a good sex drive that is not low due to improper testosterone levels. He desires and wants me!

My husband's hormones are balanced and not inhibited by any medical conditions. I pray and expect my husband's body to be healed in the name of Jesus.

There are no genetic conditions, injuries, or infections in my husband to make him have azoospermia (no sperm production).

I call forth creative miracles in my husband. Any genetic condition or injury in my husband to prevent his testes from producing sperm, I command a divine reversal in that condition and order his testes to produce sperm. I decree we will have children!

I take authority over any toxin exposure, such as pesticides, heavy metals, radiation, and industrial chemicals, and declare you will not damage sperm production.

I command my husband's sperm production to be fluent.

There is no oligospermia in my husband. My husband has abundant sperm.

My husband's varicoceles are normal in size and not enlarged in the scrotum. My husband's body is at the proper temperature, and there is no overheating of the testicles, damaging sperm production.

The tubes that carry sperm from the testes to the urethra are open. I forbid blockages. I declare everything works simply fine!

I forbid ejaculatory duct obstruction. I proclaim his sperm mixes properly with semen to exit the body.

I declare my husband's sperm are of normal shape and size.

I rebuke any doctor's diagnosis that my husband's sperm do not swim or are abnormally shaped. I thank You, Father, that You have created my husband with strong, abundant sperm, to the perfection in which You made them, and they arrive at the egg.

I forbid poor sperm motility. I declare the sperm are mobilized, swim well and reach the egg.

I prophesy and proclaim that the sperm will deliver 23 healthy chromosomes.

I come against erectile dysfunction, premature ejaculation, and retrograde ejaculation, which can affect the fertilization of an egg. I speak healing into any of these problems. I command male reproductive parts to align with the word of God and be healed, in Jesus' name. We are going to have children.

Chapter 14

Husband's Prayers for Fertility in Marriage

PRAYER DECLARATIONS

God, I ask for clear wisdom and guidance as we try to have a baby. Give me wisdom and peace in this time.

I come together in unity with my wife to pray for a baby and for our hearts' desires and dreams to happen.

Through this season of trusting You for a baby, I pray it will bring my wife and me closer together and unite us more than ever.

I rebuke any word curses or spiritual attacks that prevent us from getting pregnant.

I take authority over my sperm and my wife's eggs and declare that the right pair will fertilize each other, and my wife will get pregnant and carry the baby to full term.

I pray over my wife and say her body was made to get pregnant and carry a baby full term. I command it to happen.

I take authority over my wife, and I command that we will have a baby, in Jesus' name.

Infertility will no longer be our story. We will have a baby, in Jesus' name!

Thank You, God, for the blessing that a baby will be to my wife and me. Help us to be amazing and godly parents to our baby.

Chapter 15

Husband's Prayers for Wife, Pregnancy and Baby

Men, it is important to pray for your wife. Rebekah in the Bible was barren until Isaac, her husband, pleaded with the Lord for a child, and the Lord opened her womb. Whether for a pregnancy or infertility, you need to be involved and active in prayer for a child.

> *Now Isaac pleaded with the LORD for his wife, because she was barren; and the LORD granted his plea, and Rebekah his wife conceived.*

— Genesis 25:21

> *Your wife will be like a fruitful vine within your house; your children will be like olive shoots around your table. Yes, this will be the blessing for the man who fears the LORD.*

— Psalm 128:3-4

PRAYER DECLARATIONS

God, I ask that You give me peace in this season. Help me to trust You that this pregnancy will come to life.

God help me to put my wife's and baby's health in Your hands. Help me to trust You that they will be healthy and safe through pregnancy and delivery.

Help me to meet the needs of my wife and family in this season. Help me be the provider, leader and comforter that they need.

As the leader of my house, I take authority over this pregnancy, and I say the baby will be healthy and grow properly. I say that my wife's body will carry this baby well, and she will stay healthy and strong.

God, be with my wife and give her the strength and energy she needs to grow and deliver this baby.

Thank You, God, for this pregnancy and thank You for the life that is being made in my wife's womb. Bless my wife and our baby now.

What a joyful time this is! I will rejoice in this season and give praise to You, God.

God, help me to be the birthing partner my wife needs. Give me wisdom to know what she needs during labor. Give me the wisdom to advocate for her care and manage it as best I can.

I pray that during labor, I am relaxed and energized and that I have the energy to be with my wife and take care of her. I pray for peace and to stay healthy.

I pray, God, that Your presence is in our delivery room and that angels are looking over my wife and baby.

I ask for great godly men to come around me and help guide me through fatherhood, who can show me how to be a good, godly father.

I say I am an amazing father; I parent my child(ren) the way God has laid out in the Bible. I have the wisdom and patience I need to be an amazing father.

Section 5

First Trimester

Chapter 16

Amniotic Fluid

Amniotic fluid protects the baby during pregnancy. It nourishes the baby and helps maintain a proper temperature. Amniotic fluid plays a huge role in pregnancy and is definitely something we want to pray and declare over. It isn't merely about having amniotic fluid but having the proper amount.

The amniotic fluid level can reveal gestational diabetes or genetic and neurodevelopmental conditions in a developing fetus. Although medical professionals may tell you there is nothing that can be done, this prayer book was created so you can pray against *any* diagnosis and see healing in your baby.

Ask your doctor or midwife about your levels, and if something looks off, advocate for further testing. Take an active role in your care and your baby's health by asking questions and seeking clarity. If a result comes back abnormal, don't settle for vague answers—get the facts and pursue what is needed to protect your body and your child.

PRAYER DECLARATIONS

Heavenly Father, I thank You that my amniotic fluid is at normal levels, and I ask You to continue to protect my baby and intervene so that I maintain healthy fluid levels throughout my pregnancy.

I proclaim that the amniotic fluid will contain the correct amount of electrolytes, nutrients, hormones, and antibodies for my baby.

My fluid will have steady support and production to create a healthy placenta and material hydration.

I command the amniotic fluid to help maintain proper temperature for my baby.

I say my fluid has balance and recycling, giving good fetal kidney and lung function.

Body, Jesus said, *"I give you authority"* (Luke 10:19). Declare, "I take authority over you and say you will maintain proper fluid levels."

I declare and instruct my amniotic fluid levels to stay between 5-25cm AFI (amniotic fluid index) to protect and support my baby's development.

I take authority over my baby's fluid and speak that it stays clear without infection or meconium. It will protect my baby's breathing.

Baby, I love you. I decree you can move and exercise comfortably.

PRAYERS OF AUTHORITY OVER ADVERSE CONDITIONS

Did medical personnel say your amniotic fluid isn't normal? Let's speak over it!

I declare my amniotic fluid is (speak what it needs to be).

I rebuke word curses spoken over my amniotic fluid, in Jesus' name.

I rebuke the doctor's diagnosis (say what they told you was wrong). I speak life and health into my amniotic fluid and baby!

I forbid major leaks or premature rupture in the amniotic fluid. There will be no infection or cord compression.

Chapter 17

Umbilical Cord

The umbilical cord is the baby's lifeline. It's what gives the baby nutrients and oxygen. It connects to the placenta to nourish the baby. It helps remove waste, such as carbon dioxide. Good umbilical cord health is important, so be praying for your cord. We do want to pray over the umbilical cord as it can be life-threatening. I also want to ease your fears, too, that Lauren's son's cord was in a knot and he lived and was fine. She was a praying mama, and when she delivered, the first thing the doctor said was, "This was nothing short of the hand of God." Be a praying mama, and we will stand believing with you for God to protect your child in the womb.

PRAYER DECLARATIONS

I pray that the umbilical cord connects to the placenta properly, in Jesus' name. It will provide all the nutrients that my baby needs, in Jesus' name.

Thank You, Jesus, that the umbilical cord attaches at the center of the placenta.

I declare that the placenta is in the proper place and rebuke any placenta previa from happening.

Umbilical cord, I decree you will work properly, in Jesus' name. You will work as Jesus designed and intended for you to work. You will be strong and healthy, in Jesus' name. It is forming properly with a thick gelatinous substance inside the cord.

I say there is the proper amount of Wharton's jelly. The jelly protects the cord's blood vessels, preventing them from being compressed. I pray in the name of Jesus for the correct amount of coiling.

I pray over the umbilical cord, I say it will give life and nutrition to my baby.

I declare that the umbilical cord is delivering the correct amount of oxygen to my baby, in Jesus' name. It fills my baby's lungs and body with the proper amount of oxygen.

I command my umbilical to remove carbon dioxide and waste from my baby.

At all times, the cord will send steady oxygen and blood to my baby.

I praise You, Lord Jesus, that the umbilical cord will make sure the baby gets everything it needs for growth and development.

My baby is getting everything it needs to grow and thrive in life from the umbilical cord.

I forbid cord abnormalities. There will be no tight knots, and the cord will be the optimal size.

The cord will not be compressed and will not cut off blood flow or oxygen supply, temporarily or permanently.

I bind and restrict the cord from looping around the baby's neck.

I pray against any knots in the umbilical cord, and there will be no cord prolapse.

Chapter 18

Brain Development

I'm filled with raw emotion and a slight tear as I write this section. It is a subject I have been passionate about since I was a young adult, but it was a subject I never realized would end up in our backyard, and more so, our immediate family. Two years ago, our grandson was born with moderate brain abnormalities that would affect his entire physical body and neurodevelopment. It was a genetic condition at conception—an attack of the enemy to come against this precious life and his destiny. I want to encourage you to pray these prayers fervently. It seems this hits so many families with neuro issues, autism, and other conditions that our Heavenly Father didn't intend for our children. Cover every part of your child and your pregnancy in prayer, and make sure you drink plenty of water and get optimal protein intake, which supports brain development.

If you are reading this and you have a child already with a neurological issue, go to training.kathydegrawministries.org to join my free mentorship called Heal the Mind and Brain, where I offer specific prayers, teaching lessons, blogs, and videos to help these children and adults be healed. If God healed the man in the Gadarenes in Mark 5 of mental issues and he was sitting in his right mind (Mark 5:15), then God can also heal our children and grandchildren.

In the natural, medical practitioners would say my grandson can't be healed, but I don't live by statistics and numbers, I live by and serve a healing God that will restore all things. I will see the goodness of the Lord in the full manifestation of my grandson's healing and so many others. We are already receiving testimonies in our ministry of people with Autism and Dementia being healed, and we are just beginning to help people in this area. Pray! Do not fear! Trust God and believe!

PRAYER DECLARATIONS

I declare there will be no major genetic mutations or abnormalities during fertilization and early cell division. My baby's brain, cells, DNA, and chromosomes will form normally.

I declare full closure and proper formation of the neural tube. I command divine order into every cell.

The DNA will provide the proper instructions for how the brain should develop normally, as God created and intended.

My body produces estrogen and progesterone to support the placenta's function and protect the uterine environment. I also have healthy maternal thyroid hormone levels (T3 and T4) to support the baby's brain growth. My baby will be born alive, happy, and strong.

I will have a healthy placenta with constant oxygen and perfectly balanced hormones, and it will remove waste products from the baby's bloodstream. I forbid placental insufficiency. You will not starve my baby's brain of oxygen or nutrients. There will be no brain damage, in Jesus' name.

I order a steady supply of oxygen and nutrients; blood flow is normal, oxygen is strong, and it reaches every part of my baby, including the neural tube and developing brain regions.

Brain cells will receive a continuous supply of oxygen from the placenta. My baby's brain cells survive.

I forbid oxygen deprivation. You will not disrupt my baby's brain growth.

I have good iron levels, which support healthy red blood cells that deliver oxygen to my baby's developing brain.

I have optimal protein levels that build my baby's brain structure, including neurons, tissues, and neurotransmitters.

I declare steady growth and neurogenesis (cell formation). You will form and proceed correctly.

Brain cells, I order you to form in the right number, migrate to the appropriate places and connect to form functioning brain circuits.

I bind and restrict neural tube defects and command that there will be no neurological disruption or structural abnormality. I apply the blood of Jesus over the spine, brainstem, and neural networks.

Chapter 19

Chromosomes

od creates all babies and life in His image, which means they are
perfect and complete. God does not give sickness, congenital
disabilities, chromosome malfunctions, and other conditions that
will affect our children temporarily or permanently. He does not need to
give a child a syndrome or genetic disorder to punish the parents, use it for
His glory, or so that you have a "special" child to teach you something. It
is not God's character. He does not create a child imperfectly for a reason,
nor does He create them imperfectly at all. God is love.

The Bible clearly states we live in a fallen world where sin is, and the
enemy comes to steal, kill and destroy. (John 10:10.) Now, can God turn
what the enemy meant for evil into good? Absolutely! The Bible states that
in Genesis 50:20. And as I've said many times in this book, Romans 8:28
has been a lifeline for me in the spirit. God is working everything together
for good. He can and will use anything for His purposes, but it is important
to know that He did not cause it. I think we get stuck because we know He
is sovereign enough to prevent it, so why doesn't He intervene? We won't

know all those answers until we get to heaven. Meanwhile, we have to lift our heads, trust and praise the Lord in all things. Praise is a weapon and a truth.

I am right there with you, friend, and I speak from experience as we recently had a medically complex grandson in need of multiple miracles in his body. I know it was a direct assault from the enemy against us. Even though there are days as a Grammy that I want to cry and say it's not fair, that this should have never happened, and that it shouldn't be this way, there is also the warrior and Christ follower in me that says and knows beyond a shadow of a doubt that God will heal my grandson. Not only is He going to heal my grandchild, but He is going to heal thousands of children and adults from neurological disorders. I have to hold on to God's promises, the direction He has given me, and the words He has released to my family about healing.

If this is you and your family, I am sorry. I do know what you are going through. My advice to you is cry, grieve, mourn the loss, and have a fit if needed, then arise, fight, and target the one who truly caused this, the devil. Target him through prayers, by ministering to others, by completing your God-given assignment, and fight with everything in you to get your loved one healed and turn around your situation. We serve an awesome, mighty God, and with Him and through Him nothing shall be impossible. I am praying for you!

If you have a medically complex child, a son or daughter with a neurological condition, join my free mentorship called Heal the Mind at training.kathydegrawministries.org.

PRAYER DECLARATIONS

I take authority over the eggs and sperm, and I declare that each carries exactly 23 chromosomes, for a total of 46.

My baby will undergo the proper amount of meiosis, a cell division that creates exactly 23 pairs of chromosomes.

I bind and forbid dysfunction in meiosis. I command and order meiosis to go right, not wrong. There will be no nondisjunction, a mistake in which the chromosomes fail to separate properly.

During fertilization, a normal cell will not fuse with an abnormal cell, leading to the wrong number of chromosomes. I come against everything the enemy would come to steal, kill, and destroy in my child.

My baby will not have too few or too many chromosomes, but the perfect number of 46, each ordained by the Lord God before time. God knew this child before time. He cares for your child and wants them to be whole. *"Before I formed you in the womb I knew you; and before you were born, I sanctified you,"* (Jeremiah 1:5).

I forbid chromosomal disorders in my baby. My baby will have all their chromosomes.

I command the structure of every chromosome to be perfect. There will be no deletions, duplications, or translocations. My baby is made perfect in God's image.

I abort any mitosis errors. I command the embryo's cells to divide evenly, keeping the correct number of chromosomes.

I rebuke Trisomy 21 (Down Syndrome). You will not manifest in my unborn child.

I bind and rebuke genetic disorders. I command restoration and healing in any part of my baby, in Jesus' name.

Chapter 20

Genetics and DNA

Many details go into the formation of new life. While we can't possibly cover everything in this book and pray for everything, we do want to hit on the most important topics and have also included topics from our family experience.

God cares for us. He created us so intricately. Genetics and DNA are the starting point and building block of every baby. Right from conception, the parents' genetic material is in the sperm and egg, forming the embryo that becomes new life. Therefore, when you look at these prayers, I want you to pray them even before you begin to conceive. One of our grandsons needs a medical miracle because of what misfired at conception. It was nothing either parent did, just a fluke, I will call it a demonic attack.

If I can save one parent or one set of grandparents from going through what our family is experiencing, it will be worth it. It is difficult to see our daughter having the struggle of raising a medically complex son. I have always been passionate about using what happened to us to make sure it doesn't happen to someone else. I will. These prayers are written for my grandson, in hopes that he will begin to change lives by preventing this from happening to another family.

PRAYER DECLARATIONS

I command that I have the genetics and DNA of my heavenly Father, perfect and complete, lacking or missing nothing.

I thank You, Lord, that my baby has good genes!

My baby's DNA is formed perfectly. There will be no problems! Jesus said, "I have authority over all things." (Luke 10:19.) I take authority over his/her genes, cells, DNA, and chromosomes. There will be no deletion, duplication, mutation, or extra or missing chromosomes.

My baby's genetic instructions are copied and read correctly as my baby forms and grows.

I command that there will be no harmful mutations and that nothing will be missing in my baby's internal development.

My child will be perfect, there will be no genetic defects. I forbid it, in Jesus' name.

Chapter 21

Heart Defects

God is the strength of my heart and my portion forever.

— Psalm 73:26

A sound heart is the life of the flesh.

— Proverbs 14:30

He will strengthen your heart.

— Psalm 31:24

Don't overly concern yourself with praying for everything in this book during your pregnancy. We are trying to give you as many prayers and as much information as possible. All of my children and grandchildren were born with perfectly functioning hearts, and we did not pray these specific prayers over their hearts. The main thing is to stay in tune with the Holy Spirit; if the Lord quickens you to pray for a specific thing, pay attention and do it.

PRAYER DECLARATIONS

I bind and restrict congenital heart defects in my child. I speak and decree that there will be no structural malfunctions of my baby's heart and that it will develop properly from conception.

I bind and restrict genetic syndromes. My baby is redeemed from the curse of congenital heart defects.

I decree that the septum (wall) of my baby's heart forms accurately. He/she has optimal blood flow, with no blood leaking from the left to the right side of the heart.

I command there will be no narrowing of the aorta.

All valves, arteries, and capillaries will function as needed, be the correct size and not malfunction or be deformed, in Jesus' name.

The aorta and pulmonary arteries that leave the heart mix blood accurately and function as God intended.

My developing baby's blood flows through the heart and the rest of his/her body with perfection. I forbid holes in my baby's heart.

My baby's heart will be fully developed and will pump blood throughout the entire body.

I rebuke the enemy from coming in to steal, kill, and destroy (John 10:10) my child's life through heart defects. I declare my child has an abundant life according to Scripture.

My baby's heart is full of Jesus and beats with the rhythm of life (see Genesis 2:7).

I thank you, Father God, that my baby has a strong heart full of love for you!

I speak life, abundant health and longevity into my child!

Section 6

Second Trimester

Chapter 22

Birth Defects

I love to pray, and I learned the power of prayer. Over the years, I have witnessed praying for things and them happening, as well as things happening that I did not pray for. While I did not pray specifically over every one of my children, experience has taught me the value of covering every part of my children in prayer.

You don't have to pray these prayers daily or in a legalistic way. Don't allow yourself to fear that if you don't pray these prayers, something will happen. You need to put your trust in the Lord. We are providing prayers because we care about you. We want to help ensure you have a healthy baby. By offering prayers, we are collaborating with you in the natural to pray for the formation and health of your baby.

Don't pray out of fear. Pray out of faith. Pray every three weeks, as the Holy Spirit leads, if you feel something is off, or if a medical practitioner has told you that they are observing something in your baby which could be related to one of these prayers.

PRAYER DECLARATIONS

I bind and restrict spina bifida and command that my baby's spine will close properly.

I forbid anencephaly, where parts of the brain and skull do not form. There will be no genetic errors or environmental exposures affecting the brain and skull development of my baby.

My baby's heart beats with the rhythm of life, and there will be no congenital heart defects. I forbid it, in Jesus' name.

The heart chambers will function and form properly. There will be no hole between the heart chambers.

I declare that any medicines or pharmaceuticals that I have to take while pregnant will not have any negative impact on my baby or cause any malformation or problems. My baby will be protected from drugs.

I order all limbs to grow to full length; there will be no clubfoot, missing limbs, or parts in my child.

Kidneys, I call you forth, both of you; you will appear and develop properly.

There is no blocked urinary tract. There is no obstruction to the flow of urine.

I decree the face, mouth, lip, palate, and tongue will form properly. I rebuke any cleft lip or cleft palate.

I proclaim the tonsils and adenoids to be of normal size in my developing baby and to cause no obstruction in breathing, swallowing, eating, or sleeping.

I pronounce that the intestines will develop inside my baby's body. I restrict any holes in my baby's abdominal wall.

My baby is made perfect, and his/her esophagus connects properly to the stomach.

I declare there are no vascular issues in my baby. His/her blood flows properly during development.

Chapter 23

Failure to Thrive

FAILURE TO THRIVE: KATHY'S STORY

My daughter, Amber, was labeled as a failure to thrive at 3 months and hospitalized. She was small, and it was generational. My husband's side had a history of babies being tiny with low weight gain. The hospital did all these tests on her and wouldn't listen to our family's history, even when we had birth weights and dates from other family members' charts.

Be persistent and manage your child's health care. Don't allow them to label your child, as I did with my child. Control what tests they want you to do; it is your child. Knowing what I do now about hospitals, tests, and medical practices, I would never have allowed routine or diagnostic tests when they accomplished nothing. My child was simply small. It was genetics in the family line. I am telling you this for two reasons. I don't want you to worry if your child doesn't align with normal growth and height charts. I also don't want you to run up unnecessary medical bills or expose your child to unneeded tests, discomfort, and the side effects from some of the diagnostics. Tests are good and necessary for some cases; be educated, informed and seek guidance and wisdom. Lauren had a similar thing happen with one of her children and took a different route than we were forced to take.

FAILURE TO THRIVE: LAUREN'S STORY

When one of my kids was under a year old, I noticed they looked a little thinner than usual. I took my child in for a checkup, and that child had lost weight. My doctor diagnosed my child with failure to gain weight. The medical world labels this "failure to thrive." I can still remember standing there, taken aback, wanting to cry. We were referred to a specialist, and they wanted some testing done.

Afterward, I called my husband, and we realized why our child wasn't gaining weight—he wasn't eating enough. We worked out a feeding schedule that the doctor agreed to, and in two weeks, my child gained three pounds. He wasn't a failure to thrive; he just needed a new feeding schedule and method.

The world likes to put labels on us before even getting to know us, but our God says we are strong, we are thriving, we are alive and vibrant. He doesn't label us as failures, but as victorious. *"But thanks be to God, who gives us the victory through our Lord Jesus Christ"* (1 Corinthians 15:57).

I know there are many reasons a child might be labeled failure to thrive, and some are more serious than others. But no matter the reason, we must remember that this is not the child's identity. Their label is that they will thrive; they are strong and mighty.

One way to ensure we are not putting negative labels on our children—or even ourselves—is to avoid repeating what doctors say or the diagnoses they give. We do not claim it as ours because we are not speaking about ourselves or our child. Instead, we talk about life and health.

SPEAKING LIFE OVER YOUR CHILD

PRAYER

Jesus, help me not speak vulgar, negative, or bad language. Help me to speak life and encouragement. Let everything that comes out of my mouth be life speaking and positive.

> *Let no unwholesome word proceed out of your mouth, but only that which is good for building up, that it may give grace to the listeners.*
>
> — Ephesians 4:29

I pray that my words and thoughts are on what is true, honorable, right, pure, and lovely. That no matter what comes our way, my words and thoughts are fixed on those things.

> *Finally, brothers, whatever things are true, whatever things are honest, whatever things are just, whatever things are pure, whatever things are lovely, whatever things are of good report, if there is any virtue, and if there is any praise, think on these things.*
>
> — Philippians 4:8

God, Your will for my life and my child's life is good, pleasing, and perfect. Help me to speak life over my child. Do not let me fall into the negativity and customs of this world, but help renew my mind daily to what You say about us.

Do not be conformed to this age, but be transformed by the renewing of your mind, that you may prove what is the good and acceptable and complete will of God.

— Romans 12:2

PRAYER DECLARATIONS

I speak life over my child and baby right now, in Jesus' name.

I rebuke any word curses that have been spoken over my baby.

I rebuke any negative reports that the doctor has given about my baby.

I say that my baby is thriving, alive, and strong.

HOW TO PRAY INTO YOUR SITUATION

I realize everyone's story and journey are different. The reasons your child may be labeled with failure to thrive will vary from person to person. I know my story wasn't that severe, but it was still hard as a mom to watch and walk through. It's still hard to look at the photos of that child and see how skinny that child was.

So, whatever your story is, I want to give you some tools to help you in your journey. When you hear news like that from a doctor, immediately say, "I rebuke that, in Jesus' name." What you are saying is: "I am not receiving that report. I am taking authority over it, and that is not who my child is."

PRAYERS FOR YOUR SPECIFIC SITUATION

I rebuke the doctor's report that says _____ .

I say my child does not have _____ .

My child is not labeled _____ .

Look at your extended family. Did anyone else struggle with something similar?

If yes, then pray:

I break off any soul ties to_____ .

I rebuke generational curses of _____ .

DAILY PRAYER AND AUTHORITY

- Pray over your child as much as possible. Anoint them with prayer oil available at Kathy DeGraw Ministries. Speak life, health, and strength.
- Pick a time of day that happens every day—such as bedtime or mealtime. Hug them and rebuke the label that was put on them. Say, "I speak life and health into your body."
- Just a quick prayer during normal day activities can help you stay consistent in rebuking and taking authority over the diagnosis.
- Grandparents can join you in praying this over their grandkids. Speak life over them, too.

PRAYER DECLARATIONS

I command all genetics and generational disorders of failure to thrive to leave my bloodline and baby now, in Jesus' name.

I break the curse and generational curse of failure to thrive, in Jesus' name.

I ensure my baby receives the proper amount of protein and nutrients to thrive in utero and while breastfeeding.

My baby will develop normally. There will be no difficulty nursing, feeding, swallowing, or gaining weight. My baby will receive proper nourishment.

I bind and restrict gastrointestinal problems such as reflux, celiac disease, or diarrhea in my child. I declare there will be no metabolic disorders or food allergies.

My baby will grow and gain weight in proper proportion and at the optimal level God intended.

There will be no growth restriction or weight loss in my baby. I rebuke and take authority over any negative doctor's report.

Chapter 24

Placenta

PRAYER DECLARATIONS

I decree that my hormones are balanced and that I have adequate progesterone to stabilize the uterine lining and estrogen to promote blood vessel development and support early placental attachment and my baby's growth.

I will have proper trophoblast invasion: the cells from the embryo will burrow into the uterus and embed securely in the placenta.

Spiral arteries, known as blood vessels, will form correctly between me and my placenta. There will be perfect formation and correlation.

I will have an adequate blood supply, so my baby receives full oxygen and abundant nutrients.

I will eat plenty of folic acid, iron, calcium, magnesium, vitamin D, and omega-3 fatty acids. The nutrients I eat, and my body digests, will help support my baby's oxygen needs. The nutrients help develop a healthy placenta and support immune function. They help form my baby's healthy, complete brain, with all its components and no genetic defects.

I bind and rebuke falls, trauma, car accidents, physical abuse, and any other injury from inflicting trauma on my abdomen and causing placental abruption, miscarriage, stillbirth, congenital disabilities, or death.

Chapter 25

Preeclampsia

Preeclampsia is a serious blood pressure condition that can develop after 20 weeks of pregnancy and must never be ignored. When left untreated, it can become life-threatening for both mother and baby. This condition often comes with warning signs such as high blood pressure, headaches, blurred vision, shortness of breath, swelling or sudden weight gain, protein in the urine, and evidence of stress or damage to vital organs—most commonly the liver and kidneys.

While some mild cases can be managed medically, the reality is that the only definitive medical treatment for preeclampsia is delivery of the baby. Because of this, the condition often brings fear, uncertainty, and complex decisions during what should be a joyful season of pregnancy.

Preeclampsia also directly affects the baby by restricting blood flow and nutrients through the placenta. It can lead to decreased fetal movement, placental complications, premature birth, and increased risk to the baby's overall development and well-being.

This topic is addressed not to create fear, but to bring awareness, wisdom, and spiritual authority. Knowledge empowers you to partner with medical professionals while also standing in faith. As believers, we do not deny medical facts, but we also refuse to surrender to fear. We pray, declare, and trust God to guide every step, bring peace in the process, and cover both mother and baby with His protection, healing, and perfect will.

PRAYER DECLARATIONS

I bind and rebuke preeclampsia in my body in the name of Jesus.

Preeclampsia can't come against my baby.

I rebuke all medical diagnoses of preeclampsia, in Jesus' name.

I forbid stress, anxiety, worry, and fear causing hypertension.

I speak to my blood pressure and command it to be at normal levels for pregnancy!

I command my blood pressure to be 110/70 and my heart to beat optimally for my body.

I speak and decree that my protein level is normal.

I forbid protein in the urine. I do not and will not have proteinuria.

I command the protein levels in my urine to decrease.

I pray over my blood vessels and my baby's placenta. I command them to work in perfect harmony.

I command the placenta to be strong and function correctly. I rebuke placenta abruption, in Jesus' name.

I pray against all inflammation, and I command it to be gone!

I rebuke headaches, blurry vision, abdominal pain, nausea, vomiting, swelling from attacking me, in Jesus' name!

I do not retain excess fluid that results in swelling and edema.

My organs, including my kidneys, liver, brain, and blood, are functioning properly.

If I have symptoms of preeclampsia, I speak protection over my organs in the name of Jesus.

I restrict the formation of seizures, strokes, kidney failure, or organ damage in my body.

My baby will not have poor growth. He/she has proper blood flow to the entire body.

I decree that my baby will be of a good weight and not have weight issues.

I declare my baby will not be born prematurely, in Jesus' name!

My baby will not be a failure to thrive or have low birth weight, in Jesus' name.

I declare that there will be no long or short-term health issues for the baby related to preeclampsia.

My baby will live and not die. I speak life!

Chapter 26

Gestational Diabetes

Gestational diabetes is a type of diabetes that develops during pregnancy when the body cannot make enough insulin to meet increased demands. This can cause elevated blood sugar levels that can affect both the mother and the baby.

Gestational diabetes can increase the risk of:

- High birth weight, which may lead to difficult delivery or cesarean section
- Preterm birth
- Low blood sugar in the baby after birth
- Preeclampsia for the mother
- Higher likelihood of developing type 2 diabetes later in life (for both mother and child)

Because of these risks, women are typically monitored and given guidance on diet, blood sugar tracking, and routine testing to keep both mom and baby safe.

Be educated, ask questions, and stay informed. After walking two daughters through four pregnancies, I realized there were things I would have done differently during my own. I didn't have anyone truly guiding me, and although my mom was present, she wasn't as hands-on as I am now.

One of my biggest lessons came during the glucose test. I asked what I could eat beforehand, and they told me anything was fine. I loved juice in the morning and drank 16 ounces before consuming the glucose drink. I didn't stop to think that I was stacking sugar on top of sugar. The result was a diagnosis of gestational diabetes, which meant twice-weekly non-stress tests and pricking my finger four times a day, even though my numbers were consistently low. I was also told I would likely have gestational diabetes again, yet I didn't.

During a later pregnancy, they confirmed that I never had gestational diabetes at all. I had invested time, money, appointments, and stress into treating something that was misdiagnosed.

My reason for sharing this is simple: advocate for yourself. Ask questions, get second opinions, and make sure you fully understand what's being done and why. Staying informed helps you make the best decisions for you and your baby.

PRAYER DECLARATIONS

I break off any familiar spirit of gestational diabetes, in Jesus' name.

I break off familiar spirits and soul ties from an earlier pregnancy in which I had gestational diabetes.

I abort any gestational diabetes from manifesting in my body.

Pancreas, you will work in optimal order this entire pregnancy.

I order my pancreas to keep up with the extra demand of insulin my body needs during pregnancy.

My body will make and use insulin properly, in Jesus' name!

I order my cells to open up and receive insulin.

I order my hormones to allow insulin to move as it should and be processed.

My body regulates insulin correctly, in Jesus' name.

I command and declare that my glucose levels are in the proper range.

My fasting blood sugar will be in the normal range.

My blood sugar after I eat will be in the normal range and not spike unnecessarily.

I decree my body will process food and sugar properly.

My insulin will move sugar, glucose from the blood into my body's cells for energy, in Jesus' name.

I direct my pregnancy hormones do not interfere with insulin.

My body will work with insulin, hormones, and the placenta to maintain proper balance. I will not become insulin resistant.

My baby will process sugar and nutrients well.

I declare my baby is protected and that no negative effects can happen to them from any gestational diabetes attempting to manifest.

I rebuke any complications from gestational diabetes, in Jesus' name.

HOW TO PREVENT GESTATIONAL DIABETES

PREGNANCY (FOUNDATIONAL PREVENTION)
- Aim to begin pregnancy with a healthy, ideal weight.
- Limit refined sugar and gluten in your diet. Avoid highly processed carbohydrates such as white bread and white rice.
- Eat fruits, vegetables, and whole grains.
- Eat lean meats, such as chicken and fish, beans, and eggs.
- Incorporate healthy fats, such as avocado, olive oil, walnuts, and pecans.
- Stay physically active, walk, move, and stay healthy.

DURING PREGNANCY (ONGOING PREVENTION & MAINTENANCE)

- Maintain a healthy weight during pregnancy.
- Manage stress. Chronic stress can affect blood sugar control.

Section 7

Third Trimester

Chapter 27

Fetal Growth Restriction

LAUREN'S BIRTH STORY

In the doctor's office, I was caught off guard when I was asked, "Did the ultrasound tech say anything to you about your scan?" It was one question that could bring feelings of both fear and anxiety in an instant. It was the question we were asked after our 20-week pregnancy ultrasound. The ultrasound scan went well, but what we were not told until our OB appointment was that the baby's abdomen was measuring smaller than the rest of the baby's body.

I still remember going home after that appointment, starting to make dinner, and breaking down in tears. To hear that something might be wrong with your baby and that they are sending you to a specialist is the last thing a mother wants to hear during her pregnancy. To add to it, we couldn't get an appointment with the specialist for a couple of weeks. As difficult as it was to hear that news, I was also thankful because it gave me time to pray and decree over my body and my baby. It gave my God time to work and to heal anything that needed healing.

To be completely truthful, those weeks leading up to the appointment were not filled with doubt or depression but were filled with peace—the type of peace spoken about in Philippians 4:7. The peace that surpasses all human understanding. There were definitely moments when I struggled with difficult thoughts. Still, I knew for my baby and for my own mental state that it was extremely important for me to stay positive and take every single negative thought captive, (2 Corinthians 10:5).

We were finally able to see the maternal-fetal medicine doctor, and after a two-hour appointment, we were informed that my baby had an abdominal growth restriction. They told us about every possible negative outcome that might occur during the rest of the pregnancy and set us up for weekly monitoring to see if they could determine what was causing the growth restriction. Leaving the appointment, there was a lot to digest and process, but I stood in faith that God was going to heal my baby and that everything was going to be okay.

Now, there's a disclaimer I must say moving forward. I believe we do need medical professionals, but I also believe you have to manage your own care and do what you feel is right for you. So reluctantly, I went to weekly appointments. I knew it was what I needed to do at the moment. I wasn't sure how I felt about it because, again, I believe in managing your own care.

At the second appointment, after the doctor gave me the updated report, I looked at the doctor and said, "Where do we need to be so I do not have to see you anymore? I do not know what you believe, but I believe in God and that He can heal. What do I need to pray for?" To my surprise, the doctor was totally on board with this and believed in God, too. The doctor told me what I needed to be praying for, and that's what I did. At that point, they believed the placenta was slightly damaged, which was causing the growth restriction. I shared these things with trusted loved ones and prayer warriors because God says, "Where two or more are gathered, there He is" (Matthew 18:20).

The next months were not all butterflies and rainbows, but I tried my best to keep a positive attitude through tests and doctors' appointments. I kept my eyes on God. There were no major changes in the baby's growth restriction diagnosis. I was told they wanted to induce me at 38 weeks because, at 37 weeks, the placenta starts slowing down in function. With the placenta possibly not functioning at 100%, they wanted to get the baby out to reduce the risk of stillbirth. Yes, I said stillbirth. We knew this risk was always there—they told us at the first appointment—but we thought it was almost out of reach, far from us. But through asking questions during appointments, we found out I was considered high risk for a stillbirth.

The news of being high risk scared me a little. If the baby didn't move enough, I could feel fear starting to creep in. But in those moments, I would pray and decree over the baby, trying to change my mindset. We didn't really tell anyone about this because we didn't want it spoken into the atmosphere. We weren't going to claim that it was going to happen. We told a very select handful of people so they could pray correctly, but we didn't tell everyone because we didn't want negative words spoken. God says, *"Death and life are in the power of the tongue, and those who love it will eat its fruit"* (Proverbs 18:21), and we fully believe it. We carefully watched how we spoke about it throughout the entire pregnancy. Were we perfect all the time? Absolutely not, but we tried extremely hard to be mindful of our words.

The idea of being induced at 38 weeks was very upsetting to me. I fully believe in letting your body go into labor naturally on its own. (Disclaimer: I understand sometimes you have to be induced.) To me, this did not feel like a good reason for me to be induced. Now you may say, "But they said there was a chance of stillbirth." I am aware, but the baby had been looking great and healthy for months. Nothing looked like a good reason for an induction to me.

So, what did we do? We prayed and prayed that God would continue to heal. The entire time we were praying against having to be induced, the baby kept flipping from head down to head up. Every week was the opposite, so we prayed that the baby would be head down and stay head down and that they would be engaged in the birth canal.

Thirty-eight weeks came and went, and the baby started growing. We were thankful to hear that we could go full term—no induction. The baby turned its head down and stayed head down. Everything looked great for a natural vaginal birth, like I had been hoping and praying for. They did say, however, that if I went past 40 weeks, I would have to be induced, so again we prayed and prayed. The induction date was set, and all we could do was pray.

The day for the induction came, and my body still had not gone into labor on its own. I was a couple of days over 40 weeks, and we headed to the hospital. With tears streaming down my face, followed by a discussion of turning around and going home, we ultimately decided to head to the hospital. We started the induction process, and it did not go as we prayed it would. We hoped and prayed that my body would merely need a jump-start and then continue labor on its own, but that wasn't the case.

Labor was mentally taxing because this wasn't what I wanted it to look like. In the last two hours of labor, a lot happened, and the baby's heart rate dropped drastically. Medical staff rushed in and began working immediately. I was then told I was dilated and needed to push. When the baby came out, the doctor showed us that the baby had a knot in the umbilical cord. We were so thankful to God that the baby was healthy and safe. At that point, we did not regret going in for the induction. God knew best and had us both in His hands, watching over and protecting us.

I share my story to hopefully help someone out there—to give them hope and tools to help them through a challenging time, even if it's not pregnancy-related. So, what did I learn through this, and how can you use my story to help yourself or a loved one?

- Keep a positive mindset. Easier said than done, but even one of my doctors agreed that a positive attitude would help the baby. Babies feel everything their mothers do in the womb—joy, sadness, anger, anxiety. They feel it all; they are a part of you.
- Watch your words. Yes, you have to talk about what the doctors are saying and about reality, but be careful how you talk about it. You can say, "The doctors are saying this, but my God is the ultimate physician." Speak only about life and positivity over your situation.
- Pray. Pray. Pray. Pray over the baby as much as possible. When you feel the baby move, say, "Thank You, God, my baby is healthy." Pray Scripture and verses over your baby.
- Trust your mom instincts. If something doesn't feel right, trust that and do something about it.

- Surround yourself with a select group of people who will support you, pray for you, and speak life over your situation.
- Don't lose hope for what you want. Do you have a birth plan? Call it forth. Pray for it and believe it will come to pass.
- Manage your health care. Ask questions. Get answers. They will help you understand what's going on and give you directions on what to pray.

PRAYER DECLARATIONS

My body works properly, and every organ and female reproductive part supplies my baby with normal levels of oxygen, nutrients and blood flow during pregnancy.

I bind and rebuke placental insufficiency and abruption. If there is any malfunction or deficiency in my placenta, I call you to order right now and require that you perform accordingly.

I restrict preeclampsia from attacking my body. I will not have high blood pressure. There will be no damage to the small blood vessels in the placenta. I take authority over you and command my body to align with the word of God.

I forbid diabetes, kidney disease, autoimmune diseases and infections from causing growth restrictions. Any attacks of these things manifesting in my body, I command them to leave my body right now and for my body to come into order.

I order stress, anxiety, worry, and fear to leave my body. I command that stress will not impact the blood flow to my baby. I live in peace and rest, not stress. *"You will keep him in perfect peace, whose mind is stayed on You, because he trusts in You"* (Isaiah 26:3).

My child is formed with perfectly functioning organs: his/her heart, brain, and kidneys function normally. There are no congenital disabilities in my baby because I take authority over my baby and decree that defects will not manifest in my child.

I decree my baby will grow at a normal rate inside the womb.

I forbid growth restriction or for my baby to be diagnosed as smaller than expected for his/her gestational age.

My baby is growing properly. I say nothing is restricting his/her growth. No root cause or underlying problem is preventing my baby from developing properly.

I declare my baby will have proper oxygen levels at birth and will not have hypoglycemia.

PROTIPS

- Eat plenty of protein, healthy fats, vitamins and minerals.
- Drink water and stay hydrated.
- Get adequate sleep.
- Stop alcohol, smoking and drugs.
- Seek medical attention for any viral infection during pregnancy.

Chapter 28

Stillbirth

*Now faith is the substance of things hoped for, the evidence of
things not seen.*

— Hebrews 11:1

To the moms, dads, and families out there who have experienced
stillbirth, I am so sorry. To those whom doctors have labeled as
high risk for stillbirth, we understand, because I, (Lauren), was
thus labeled by doctors. But we are not our labels, and our babies are not
what the world labels them. We don't always understand what is
happening inside the womb, but God is with us through it all.

If you have experienced a stillbirth or a miscarriage, I want to
encourage you to get, Kathy's book, *Unshackled*. I have helped women
work through the grieving process, and I have a very thorough protocol to
be able to help you find peace.

Unshackled along with Kathy's other books are available on Amazon. QR code to link you to her books!	

I want to assure you that your child is in heaven. When I had a miscarriage, the Lord revealed my baby in heaven. I was interviewed on a television program about my encounter in heaven.

You can watch my 10-minute interview describing me seeing my son in heaven by scanning the QR code.	

We are speaking life into your situation. Years ago, the Lord connected me with another ministry for those experiencing stillbirth during pregnancy or at birth. Please connect with them immediately upon diagnosis or death for a special care package and healing help.

Angels in Waiting Ministry help and healing for those experiencing the loss of a baby in, before or shortly after birth.	

HEALING PRAYER FOR STILLBIRTH (CAN BE APPLIED TO MISCARRIAGE.)

Heavenly Father, I am hurting and sad. I don't want to stay in loss or grief. I declare I trust You even when I don't understand. I pray You will take care of my child and heal my broken heart. I know You didn't intentionally leave me here hurting and in pain. I know all things are in Your hands. I will have faith. I will heal. I will live again internally. I will live for my family. I will live for myself, and I will live for the children who live now in heaven, in true life. I leave my tears at the feet of Jesus, and I move forward knowing that I serve a sovereign Lord who loves me and my child abundantly.

There are many reasons why a baby might be stillborn, such as umbilical cord issues, placental issues, infections, genetics and many other reasons. But sometimes we don't understand why, and there is nothing we could have done to prevent it.

WE SERVE A REDEEMING GOD

If you are not familiar with the story of Cain and Abel in the Bible, they were the sons of Adam and Eve. One day, Cain killed Abel and years later, Eve gave birth to another son (Seth) for Adam, which was a gift since he lost one son.

Adam had relations with his wife again, and she had another son and called his name Seth, for she said, "God has granted me another offspring instead of Abel, because Cain killed him."

— Genesis 4:25

No one is replaceable, so please don't take that away from what I am saying. What I want to show you here is that God gave Adam and Eve another son after they had lost one.

If you have experienced a miscarriage or stillbirth, I am sharing this to give you hope that even though that loss can never be replaced, God can give you more children if that's what you desire.

PRAYER FOR YOU!

God, I thank You for every woman and family member reading this who has experienced a stillbirth or whose pregnancy has been labeled high risk for stillbirth by medical professionals. I pray peace over them. I pray that You give them hope, faith, and an unending peace that consumes them.

For those babies who are still in their mommies' tummies, we speak life over them. High risk and stillbirth are not their labels. They are labeled healthy and whole—righteous, loved, and chosen. They are full of life and strength. Their bodies and wombs are made whole and healthy.

We pray strength over the mom's body and command her body to carry this baby healthily and to full term. We pray that her body will be a place of peace and comfort for the baby to grow properly and in accordance with God's perfect image.

God's faithfulness is with mom and baby. He will *strengthen* them together as a unit, bringing forth health and wholeness.

You got this, momma! Don't give up hope!

For I have said, "Mercy will be built up forever; Your faithfulness will be established in the heavens."

— Psalms 89:2

My frame was not hidden from You, when I was made in secret, and skillfully wrought in the lowest parts of the earth.

— Psalms 139:15

PRAYER DECLARATIONS

I bind and rebuke a spirit of death over my child. My baby will live and not die and declare the works of the Lord, (Psalms 118:17).

My placenta will work properly until after birth when I deliver it. It will not separate prematurely, cutting off oxygen and nutrients to my baby; I take authority over it right now.

I forbid cord prolapse. The cord will not have knots or cord compression.

I restrict the cord from wrapping tightly around my baby's neck. I take authority over the cord and declare that you will cause no birth defects or death.

I bind and restrict infections in my body and the baby. No infection, you hear me, no infection will cross the placenta, causing stillbirth.

I decree that any preexisting health conditions that I have been diagnosed with will not affect the birth and life of my baby.

All the organs in my baby are properly formed and completely functional. There are no developmental problems in my baby's organs.

I rebuke and annihilate any chromosomal abnormalities; you will not exist, and any chromosomal dysfunction, absence, or defect will not cause death! I forbid it.

If any fetal growth restriction has been present or diagnosed, I speak to you and say, turn around.

My baby will overcome any deficiency and grow to the proper gestational size. No health complications I have experienced or been diagnosed with will cause stillbirth. I rebuke medical statistics and facts that my baby is at a higher risk of death.

HOW THE PLACENTA AND UMBILICAL CORD WORK TOGETHER

A healthy umbilical cord contains three blood vessels:

One umbilical vein, which transports oxygen-rich blood from the placenta to the fetus.

Two umbilical arteries, which transport oxygen-poor blood from the fetus back to the placenta.

Now, let's tie this into a Scripture that we can declare on behalf of our baby.

And if someone might overpower another, two people can withstand him. A threefold cord is not quickly broken.

— Ecclesiastes 4:12

PRAYER

I declare that my baby's cord consists of three vessels. Each vessel works in perfect unity as God designed. The three vessels will function perfectly and sustain my baby. The cord transports blood and oxygen smoothly and properly, in Jesus' name. These three vessels will not malfunction or be disrupted in their duties. God, You have heard my prayers and decrees. I ask You to cover my baby's umbilical cord and placenta with Your hand of protection. Keep it working properly and strong. Help it to nourish my baby's body and help my baby to grow, in Jesus' name. Amen!

Chapter 29

Baby's Positioning

The last trimester is when you should start praying for your baby's positioning. It is normal for the baby to move, be in the proper position, turn, and then get out of the position in which they should deliver. There will be variations; therefore, it is important in the third trimester to keep these prayers present and in front of you and consider praying them weekly, so your baby is in the proper position for a healthy vaginal delivery.

PRAYER DECLARATIONS

My body releases relaxin, the hormone necessary towards the end of pregnancy to soften the ligaments and joints of the pelvis to make it wider for the baby to come out with ease during birth. Relaxin releases to soften my cervix.

My baby's head drops lower in the pelvis, facing my spine and stays in the position. He/she will not turn or be born breech.

I will not need intervention for my baby's position. My baby will be in the proper position for an easy labor without unnecessary medical intervention.

I say my body will have increased uterine sensitivity because my estrogen is making my body more responsive to oxytocin.

I call forth proper engagement and lightning. It will come at the appropriate time.

Section 8

Labor and Delivery

Chapter 30

Labor and Delivery

A woman giving birth to a child has pain because her time has come; but when her baby is born she forgets the anguish because of her joy that a child is born into the world.

— John 16:21

In this chapter, we break down three sets of labor and delivery prayer declarations. As mentioned earlier, this book was birthed from our time in a labor and delivery room with Lauren's third child. I was primarily there as an in-room intercessor, which I highly suggest for everyone. For Lauren's first child, I was told to sit in the corner and pray. I was instructed to stay out of the way, allow them privacy and to not interject unless asked for wisdom and advice. I gladly agreed to be the prayer covering as they delivered their first child. If you have a trusted prayer warrior, I would encourage you to invite them along. I had to fervently pray for three of my grandchildren when challenges began to arise and even had to wage war for some of their lives.

Lauren's doctor was the same for all three children. I remember the first time I was in the delivery room with them. The doctor loved that I was praying. I always prayed audibly, but I did it in a lower voice to avoid being a distraction to what was happening. The doctor at one point said, "You can pray louder!" She welcomed the prayer. Therefore, in the birth of her last child, when things were not progressing, I began to ask the doctor what to pray specifically and got out my notebook. I am glad to be able to provide this first set of labor and delivery declarations with medical insights that we received in the room as we were birthing a baby through prayer. I encourage you to purchase this book for your prayer partners and moms so they know how to pray precisely while you are in labor.

PRAYER DECLARATIONS FROM ACTIVE LABOR AND DELIVERY

How exciting! If this book helped you get to this point, send a testimony to: testimonies.kdministries@gmail.com. We would also love to pray for you on this journey!

SPIRITUAL COVERING

I plead the blood of Jesus over the mother and baby.

The abundance of angels surround this delivery process and room (or home).

I dispatch angels to assist in this delivery process with ease.

I go in the strength of the Lord, (Psalm 71:16).

I am able and abounding to deliver a healthy baby naturally in the strength of the Lord.

HORMONAL FLOW

I command hormonal imbalances to be bound and restricted.

I am thankful progesterone levels are dropping, preparing my body for labor.

My body is capable of adapting to the hormonal changes necessary for delivery.

Oxytocin has an abundant overflow in the body.

We summon an increase in oxytocin. We command abundant, steady flow of oxytocin.

I thank You for an active flow of oxytocin.

I say anywhere oxytocin is held up, I order it to release, in Jesus' name.

FETAL SIGNALING

The baby releases fetal signals to mom as a sign of labor progression and readiness.

I call forth elevated fetal signals to produce proper changes in the uterus and cervix.

I proclaim a natural acceleration with no pharmaceuticals or intervention.

CERVICAL RESPONSE & DESCENT

I say my body engages properly to put pressure on the cervix, and the cervix responds by dilating.

I say the baby's head drops into the pelvis and puts pressure on the cervix, causing the cervix to thin, soften, open, widen, and ripen.

CONTRACTIONS & PROGRESSION

My uterus contracts with intensity and consistency.

There will be no delays or stalls in contractions.

I evoke progression in labor, contractions, and delivery.

I command progression in labor and contractions.

I bind and restrict enemy attacks and self-invited tension and pressure.

I command the body to accelerate in delivery.

CONTRACTION EFFECTIVENESS

I command every contraction to perform its duties.

I command every contraction to produce the proper response in the body, uterus, and cervix.

I decree agility on the contractions, in the name of Jesus—agility to move quickly and easily, especially when accelerating.

ENDURANCE

I speak that the birth mother will not grow tired or weak, but will go forth in the strength of the Lord.

I pray for exponential movement, growth, and progression in labor.

I thank You every word, prayer, and declaration is going forward and producing results. Every word is being sent forth into the atmosphere and spiritual realm to manifest a natural result and manifestation.

LAUREN'S PERSPECTIVE ON LABOR AND DELIVERY:

Labor and delivery—I, (Lauren), believe you either look forward to it or dread it. Call me strange, but I love the labor and delivery part. There is no other feeling than knowing you worked and labored to bring a baby into this world. Feeling the baby crown and come out (if having a vaginal birth) is unlike any other experience. I strongly encourage women to experience this, if possible, at least once in their lives.

You can probably guess already, but I am one of those "crazy" people who believe in 100% natural labor and delivery. I do want to add that I believe there is a time and place for medical intervention. If natural labor and delivery is your goal and dream, I am praying and believing you get it. If it's not your dream or goal, or it's not in the cards for you, I agree and pray that whatever your dream labor and delivery experience is, you get that.

If you are hoping for natural, glory-filled labor and delivery, I highly recommend the book *"Childbirth in the Glory"* by Janet Mills. I am going to be honest—I read this book for my last birthing experience, and I didn't get the labor I dreamed and prayed for. However, the book helped me mentally prepare for whatever was thrown my way. It encouraged me and gave me peace through the birth I did have.

QR Code to book by Janet Mills *Childbirth in the Glory*

PRAYER

I pray that God hears your prayers for your labor and delivery, that whatever birthing experience you desire, He grants you the desires of your heart. I pray your labor and delivery will be easy, pain-free, and quick. I pray your baby will be in the proper position and remain healthy before, during, and after birth. I pray your body heals and responds well to labor and delivery, and that God gives you peace.

PRAYER DECLARATIONS FOR LABOR AND DELIVERY

My body is preparing for labor and delivery.

My hormones are doing the job God designed them to do.

My body will make relaxin, the hormone that helps my muscles relax and become flexible, so my baby can come out.

Prostaglandins will be produced to help ripen my cervix and initiate contractions.

I command my cervix to thin and soften for labor.

My baby engages in my pelvis over my cervix.

When my baby is ready, he/she will signal my body to go into labor.

My body will produce oxytocin to help trigger and maintain labor.

I will have the proper amount of oxytocin to go into labor naturally and birth this baby naturally.

I am at peace and hopeful for my delivery. I bind anxiety that triggers adrenaline. Anxiety and adrenaline will not slow down my labor and delivery process.

I command the rupture of membranes and for my water to break naturally and at the proper timing during labor. It will not happen before and cause premature labor during my pregnancy. I decree that I will not need medical intervention to have my membranes ruptured.

I proclaim that the rupture of my amniotic sac releases fluid and helps accelerate contractions and labor naturally and without medical intervention.

Oxytocin will strengthen uterine contractions.

The uterus will contract to cause contractions that help push my baby out.

I will have a smooth and easy delivery.

I will be strong in labor.

My body will relax, helping contractions not be painful and my baby to come down and out.

God designed my body to birth this baby naturally.

I am capable of birthing this child naturally.

God will be with me every step of the way.

My mind will stay positive. Distractions will not prevent me from birthing this baby calmly and naturally.

The Lord is my strength; through Him all things are possible.

SCRIPTURE FOR PEACE AND STRENGTH

I have the mind of Christ.

— 1 Corinthians 2:16.

The Lord is my strength and my shield; my heart trusted in Him, and I was helped; therefore my heart rejoices, and with my song I will thank Him.

— Psalms 28:7

I can do all things, because of Christ who strengthens me.

— Philippians 4:13

Cast all your care upon Him, because He cares for you.

— 1 Peter 5:7

Now may the Lord of peace Himself give you peace always in every way. The Lord be with you all.

— 2 Thessalonians 3:16

Ask and it will be given to you; seek and you will find; knock and it will be opened to you.

— Matthew 7:7

LAUREN'S STORY

I am not going to go into deep detail about my birth experiences because I don't want to be just another great or not-so-great birth story for you to hear. But I do want to share some of my story to encourage you.

As you may have already figured out, I am all for natural births. For me, that means unmedicated, vaginal delivery—the way our bodies were created to give birth. That said, this was not my story for all my births. I have experienced natural births, and I have experienced medicated births as well.

With each birth, I prayed more intentionally, knowing what I needed to pray for and how to pray. I took natural birthing classes and researched how to manage discomfort and the mental challenges of labor.

I had one beautiful, easy birth—it was exactly what I prayed for and envisioned. I also had one that was not. I prayed throughout the pregnancy, envisioned the birth, and declared over my body and baby daily, yet I did not get the birth I wanted. I literally cried during labor because of it.

I don't share this to discourage you, but to be real and honest. Sometimes we do not get exactly what we pray for, and sometimes we don't know why. Was our faith too little? Did we not pray enough? We may never know. We live in a fallen world, and sometimes, no matter how hard we pray, situations still happen.

Were all my prayers answered exactly the way I wanted? No. But I believe what happened was best. Preparing myself spiritually helped me through the mental battle. It kept my mind focused on God and helped me know what to do in the hard moments. Many prayers were answered—my baby was healthy, I was healthy, I had a vaginal delivery, pushing was easy, and I got to feel my baby come out.

I say all of this to say that I stand with you, believe in your vision, and agree with these prayers coming forth. But know this—you are not alone if every prayer does not come forth exactly the way you hoped.

PRACTICAL TIPS FOR LABOR AND DELIVERY

- Set the room. Dim the lights, play music, and have your comfort items ready and accessible.
- Earplugs can help block out noise and allow you to focus on laboring.
- Relax. The more you relax your body and let contractions occur, the less painful they are.
- Try various positions. Having a doula or a nurse who knows how to support labor and suggest positions can help labor progress more smoothly and quickly.
- I highly recommend Janet Mills's *Childbirth in the Glory* to prepare for labor and delivery.

- If you want to take a class, Karen Welton's *Pain-Free Birth* is also a good option.

PRAYER DECLARATIONS - LABOR PROGRESSION

My labor will develop normally. I will not fail to progress or receive a labor dystocia diagnosis.

I will have a natural childbirth. There will be no unnecessary intervention. I declare a normal delivery without Pitocin or a C-section.

My baby will be head down, facing my spine, chin tucked.

I restrict cord prolapse. My umbilical cord will not come before my baby.

The umbilical cord will not be wrapped around my baby's neck. I restrict the spirit of death.

There will be no cord compression. My baby will receive the proper amount of oxygen.

I speak life into my baby. There will be no fetal distress, oxygen deprivation, or abnormal heart rate patterns.

My baby will have a steady, strong oxygen supply during labor and delivery.

I command my placenta to provide uninterrupted oxygen and nutrients through the umbilical cord, in Jesus' name.

My contractions will be normal and not compromise oxygen flow.

I declare a strong fetal heart rate between 110 and 160 beats per minute.

I forbid late decelerations and any distress.

There will be no placental abruption or umbilical cord prolapse.

My baby's shoulders will not get stuck behind my pubic bone. I forbid shoulder dystocia.

My baby will tolerate labor well and recover fully between contractions.

There will be no stress on my baby.

My labor will progress steadily without infection or oxygen deprivation.

I will not need an emergency C-section.

I restrict postpartum hemorrhage. I will not have complications or life-threatening bleeding.

My baby will breathe effectively within the first 30 seconds of birth, with clear lungs and healthy circulation.

As my body prepares to deliver my baby in God's perfect timing, I declare:

- Progesterone levels decrease appropriately.
- Estrogen levels rise, making my uterus sensitive to contractions.
- The pituitary gland releases oxytocin to strengthen contractions.
- Prostaglandins increase to ripen and thin my cervix.
- Cervical effacement progresses smoothly.
- My cervix opens with ease, without tearing or trauma.

Chapter 31

APGAR

One thing I want to say to you is, do not worry. Don't allow yourself to immediately think about the worst-case scenario when going through labor and delivery. My son is now 32 years old and is alive and healthy. However, my son was born under fetal destress and came out two on the APGAR with the next score being a six. He was able to recover, and I declare that for your child too, if a situation should arise.

Shortly after your baby is born, medical staff or a midwife will evaluate your baby and give the baby an APGAR score. But what is an APGAR score? APGAR stands for:

Appearance (color), Pulse (heart rate), Grimace (relaxation ability), Activity (muscle tone), and Respiration (breathing effort). You want a score between 7 and 10. If the baby has a lower score, medical treatment may be recommended. The APGAR score is assessed at several-minute intervals to give the baby a chance to improve and respond.

PRAYER

I speak over my baby right now and say he/she will have a good APGAR score. The score will be within the normal range, and nothing can affect my baby's score. My baby will be active, breathing, well-colored, and have a good heart rate. Jesus, I thank You that my baby will have a good APGAR score. Amen.

PRAYER DECLARATIONS

Any meds given to me during labor will not affect my baby's APGAR score.

I forbid birth trauma, and if there are complications, it will not affect my baby's APGAR score.

I speak over my baby, and I command you to have a great APGAR score!

My baby's APGAR score will be between 7 and 10! You are thriving and vibrant! Your appearance is healthy and beautiful!

Baby, I love you! Your heart rate is normal range for a newborn.

My baby's heart will beat faster than one hundred times per minute at birth.

I declare the muscle tone is healthy and well-developed. It has flexed arms and legs.

My baby's grimace ability is active and well reactive! My baby cries!

I declare that the moment my baby comes out, you take deep breaths. Your lungs are fully developed!

Respiration is strong; he/she breathes on his/her own and has the breath of life! His/her cries are abundant, and he/she can take in oxygen to cry.

I proclaim my baby's appearance will be pink all over and full of life!

Chapter 32

Breech Baby

A breech baby is not in the proper position for natural birth, which is head down and face facing the mother's back.

LAUREN'S STORY

I, (Lauren), had weekly ultrasounds during one of my pregnancies, and the baby looked great. His position was good up until 36 weeks, when my baby flipped. They were talking about inducing me at 38 weeks due to health concerns with my baby. I knew that if the baby did not flip, that would mean a C-section. (I am aware that babies are born breech vaginally all the time and are okay.) However, not all doctors and midwives will deliver that way. You have to know what's best for you and your baby. I wasn't sure trying for a breech vaginal delivery was the best decision for my baby, given the high-risk pregnancy I had been diagnosed with.

The news of the baby being flipped definitely worried me and was hard for me. Everything else in that pregnancy wasn't going as I had planned. I had been praying for my baby, and now to be looking at a possible cesarean was the icing on top. I didn't let it weigh me down, though. I envisioned and believed my baby would flip. I kept imagining having a pain-free, natural labor filled with God's presence. I believed God could flip my baby again. I kept on praying this prayer from *Birthing in the Glory*: "My baby is head down and face down." That was my prayer. I went in for my next appointment, and praise God, my prayer was answered—the baby had flipped.

However, the fight wasn't over. I had appointments twice a week, and when I tell you the baby flipped back and forth between each appointment, I am not kidding you. We waited in anticipation for three to four weeks to see if the baby was going to be head down or not. Thank You, Jesus, the baby stayed head down, and around 39 weeks, I was able to deliver vaginally.

PRAYER DECLARATIONS

I command my placenta to be in the proper position. You will not prevent my baby from being head down.

Uterus, make room for my baby to move into the head-down position and then stay there.

Baby, you are dropping head down and face down into my pelvis to stay head down till birth.

BREECH BABY PRAYERS

If your baby is going to be born breech, here are some prayers to pray over the baby:

My baby has great cognitive abilities.

My baby will not have a cleft lip or palate.

My baby will not have hip dysplasia. My baby's hips are in the proper position and will stay there.

My baby will not have any trauma from birth.

My baby will come out easily, in Jesus' name.

BREECH BABY HELPS

If your baby is predicted to be breech, there are some things besides prayer that you can do to try to help the baby flip.

- Do internet research on Spinning Babies.
- Seek out a doula or midwife. They can be trained in Spinning Babies and can help you naturally flip the baby.
- Fascial massage along with Spinning Babies (This is what I was going to do. I had appointments scheduled, but the baby flipped, so obviously I didn't need to go.)

Seek medical wisdom from your doctor. There is a manual flip called ECV (External Cephalic Version). Do your research and ask thorough questions before proceeding. I asked the following questions, which you can use if needed:

- What is the success rate?
- How painful is it?
- If needed, what pain medications are given?
- What stress does it put on the baby?
- If it doesn't work, then what?
- What if something goes wrong?

Always educate yourself before doing something. If you see a chiropractor or doula for Spinning Babies, ask about the risks and success rates. If you are having a high-risk pregnancy or have complications during pregnancy, make sure to mention that and address it before proceeding.

Chapter 33

Cesarean Section

We understand it is every woman's dream and God's natural design for us to have a natural childbirth. We truly hope and pray it happens for you. However, I want to encourage and talk to those for whom it may not be possible for a natural birth due to your health, your baby, or simply because it doesn't work out that way in the end.

The bottom line is we want live births and healthy babies. Ultimately, how we get there does not matter. There is no shame or condemnation if it doesn't work out that way for you. I know for Lauren it was particularly important to avoid a C-section, but for my daughter, Amber, she was at peace with a C-section. They took different paths to delivery, but neither was wrong nor should be judged.

I want to tell you my story in hopes of helping someone make a decision. My first delivery was vaginal. I had a long, hard labor, with my epidural wearing off, my son pinching a nerve in my leg, causing excruciating pain, and in the end, he was stuck in my birth canal, and they had to grab him out with forceps because he was in fetal distress. He was resuscitated twice at birth and was two on the APGAR when born, which is very severe. The bottom line was that my birthing canal (vagina) was too narrow. He was only seven pounds, so not too big.

My doctor gave me the choice on the following pregnancies, whether I wanted to attempt a vaginal birth again or if I desired to elect for a C-section due to the delivery complications. Friends, it was an easy decision for me. I was going with the C-section. The thought of possibly having another child get stuck, die, or have to leave them in the hospital after I went home without my son, I was not going to take a chance.

I have a saying, "Be you; everyone else is taken." Be you with your labor and delivery decisions and do what is best for you physically and mentally, and ultimately whatever will get you a live birth and healthy baby. There is no shame in taking a different path than another person if it is what is best and needed for you and your baby.

PRAYER DECLARATIONS

God, I ask You to be with me and give me unexplainable peace and trust while preparing for the C-section and during it.

I pray for Your glory and peace to be in that operating room.

I pray for wisdom over the surgeon, nurses and anesthesiologist. Anoint their hands with Your glory, God.

I pray that my cesarean section will go well and with ease, in Jesus' name.

There will be no pain during my C-section.

There will be no adverse effects from anesthesia.

There will be no complications involved with my C-section, in Jesus' name.

I pray that my baby will maintain proper vital levels during the C-section.

The baby will be lifted out of my womb with ease.

God, help me to still get a boost of oxytocin and that golden-hour bonding moment.

Every layer of my skin regenerates completely, restoring strength and elasticity.

I will have no scars or scar tissue.

Recovery will be easy with minimal to no pain.

Section 9

Breastfeeding and Milk Supply

Chapter 34

Breastfeeding

THE GIFT OF CONNECTION

But You are He who took me out of the womb; You kept me safe on my mother's breasts.

— Psalms 22:9

Oxytocin, often called the "love hormone," is released when your baby nurses. It causes your milk to let down and also strengthens the bond between mother and baby. I, (Lauren), always enjoyed nursing time as a chance to connect with my baby.

We can get so busy as moms during the day. Having those nursing moments to slow down, connect, and be with your baby is truly a gift. God designed our bodies to produce milk and nourish our babies. There are so many health benefits if you can breastfeed your baby. Even if you cannot breastfeed for a full year, any amount of time breastfeeding can have lasting benefits.

Can I, (Kathy), be honest with you? I had no desire to breastfeed my first child. I was a working mom and didn't know how I would manage it. I heard horror stories about breastfeeding—how much work it was and how long it took for you and your baby to develop a rhythm.

When I got pregnant with my second child, something in my heart changed. I had the desire to try. I nursed for about a week, but I had to stop because my baby wasn't getting the nutrients she needed due to several factors. Looking back, it actually turned out to be what she needed. She was small and was later labeled as having failure to thrive, and we needed to measure exactly how much milk she was getting.

At the time, we also didn't have lactation consultants or the breastfeeding support available today. If you want to breastfeed or are having difficulties, please take advantage of the free breastfeeding services that are available now.

When I had Lauren, I wanted to breastfeed so badly. I prayed and prayed and prayed that I would be able to breastfeed, that we would have an instant bond and rhythm, and that it wouldn't take six weeks like everyone said it would.

You know what I got for all that prayer? My baby latched instantly, breastfed beautifully, and never took more than ten bottles her entire life. I had no adjustment period, no mastitis, and no other challenges. She nursed perfectly—so well, in fact, that she would rather cry than take a bottle if I weren't home.

I believe in the power of prayer. I prayed for this experience, and while I understand that not everyone will have the same outcome, I still encourage you to pray if breastfeeding is the desire of your heart. Remove the naysayers. Guard your heart. Pray for what you are believing.

LAUREN'S PERSPECTIVE ON BREASTFEEDING

Breastfeeding is a gift God has created for mothers. I, (Lauren), feel like breastfeeding has this fairy-tale expectation—that it is easy, pain-free, comes naturally, and is an intimate bonding time. I pray that that is your experience. The reality is that it can be a journey. Everyone's journey is different. For some, it's harder than others, but in the end, it is so rewarding.

I want to make this as positive and uplifting as I can, but I also want to be real with you. I am putting my journey of breastfeeding at the end of this chapter because I want to share my raw, honest experience.

PRAYERS DECLARATIONS

God created my body to feed my child, and it will work as He designed it to.

My body is capable of breastfeeding my baby.

Jesus, I ask that my breastfeeding experience would be glory-filled, full of connection, life, and peace.

I pray my baby will not have tongue-tie or feeding issues.

I pray that breastfeeding will be easy for my baby and me. My baby will have no issues latching, in Jesus' name.

My baby will suck and latch well.

Breastfeeding will not be painful, in Jesus' name.

Breastfeeding is fun and easy.

I speak to my breasts and say they will produce the proper amount of milk for my baby.

My milk will be rich with nutrients.

My baby will get all the nutrients he/she needs from breastfeeding.

I will have a milk supply for as long as I choose to breastfeed.

My baby and I will bond as we nurse.

Find a time of day to declare these truths. While doing dishes, driving, or showering, say, "Breastfeeding will be easy," or, "I will nurse my child with joy and ease." Praying audibly is important, as I've mentioned earlier.

To those of you reading this who have already had a child, how was your breastfeeding experience? Good? Bad? Let's make it better this time.

If you have struggled in the past, pray specifically against those struggles.

I say we will not have _____ .

I will not struggle with _____ .

My baby will not struggle with _____ .

Also, renew your mindset. Do not go into this experience expecting the same outcome as before. Go into it with faith and a renewed mind.

LAUREN'S BREASTFEEDING JOURNEY (RAW AND HONEST):

I warned you—this is my journey and my raw feelings.

Breastfeeding hurts at first. It is unpleasant, and even after a couple of days, it can still hurt. Nipples that are not used to that kind of use can become raw, blistered, and even bloody. It can be toe-curling, teeth-clenching pain in the beginning. Pumping hurts, too. I remember the first time I used a pump—I wanted to cry.

I have been blessed to nurse each of my children, although one of my kids was not the ideal breast feeder, with the gymnastic type of movements and thrashing around. One breastfeeding journey was definitely more difficult than the others. Just two weeks postpartum, I got mastitis. I treated it, but things still didn't feel right. I later found out I had a yeast infection from the antibiotics given during birth. I treated that, but I got mastitis again because yeast infections can cause it. Within twelve weeks postpartum, I had yeast infections twice and mastitis three times. It was a rough season, but I'm so glad I pushed through and kept breastfeeding.

On another journey, breastfeeding itself went well, but my baby wasn't getting enough nutrients. I had to switch to pumping so we could measure intake. Even through these struggles, I breastfed most of my babies until they were a year old. It's not always easy, but it is rewarding and incredibly healthy for them.

Engorgement when your milk comes in is extremely uncomfortable. It can feel like you have two melons attached to you. Add in mastitis, yeast infections, or latch issues, and it can feel overwhelming. But here's the good news—if you can persevere, it does get better. I've found that if you can make it through the first 8–12 weeks, you and your baby usually settle into a rhythm.

PRACTICAL BREASTFEEDING TIPS

I am not a professional—these are simply things I learned along the way:

PREPARATION (BEFORE BABY ARRIVES)

- Invest in comfortable nursing bras and nursing-friendly clothes.
- Use bra pads to protect from leaks; reusable ones work well.

EARLY BREASTFEEDING (FIRST DAYS–WEEKS)

- A proper latch usually means the baby's tongue is over the bottom gums and teeth.
- Use nipple cream to help prevent cracked or bloody nipples.
- Change wet bra pads and air out breasts to help prevent yeast infections. If you've taken antibiotics, consider a probiotic.
- If something feels off—pain, latch issues, soreness—find a lactation consultant.

MILK IN / ENGORGEMENT STAGE

Engorgement is uncomfortable but temporary. Hot showers or baths can help; hand-express carefully for relief.

POSSIBLE COMPLICATIONS

Mastitis is a breast infection that can occur (watch for symptoms and treat promptly).

HORMONAL DECLARATIONS FOR BREASTFEEDING

I speak to my body and hormones, commanding them to rise and function properly.

I declare the growth of milk ducts and milk-producing cells.

After delivery, prolactin takes over, stimulating milk production.

I command oxytocin to release during nursing, causing proper let-down and milk flow through the ducts to my nipples.

Chapter 35

Mastitis

Mastitis is an infection of breast tissue. Mastitis is not pleasant at all. I pray you never have to experience it, but if you do, I hope what I am about to say helps. Mastitis can make you feel like you have the flu—headache, fever, chills, nausea, and other symptoms. Redness and tenderness of the breast are big signs. Mastitis occurs when a milk duct is blocked, a yeast infection develops in the nipples, or there is an oversupply of milk. These are the most common causes.

BLOCKAGE IN A MILK DUCT

To help prevent this, make sure you empty your breast during a feeding or pumping session. Don't go too long between pumping or feeding, and don't miss one.

LAUREN'S STORY

I have gotten mastitis twice from learning this lesson the hard way. The first time, I didn't finish a pumping session because my baby woke up, so I just nursed them instead. The second time, I was busy doing a household task and went too long between feedings.

TREATMENT OPTIONS

I am going to be honest with you—in my opinion, treatment for mastitis is based on what works for your body. I have been told different ways to treat this by medical professionals.

- Apply a hot compress to the breast and do extra pumping or hand expression to try to work the clog out.
- Apply a cold compress and let the breast rest, even skipping a pumping or feeding on that side. The idea behind this method is that mastitis is an inflammatory condition, so you treat it with cold and rest.
- Epsom salt soaks can also help, along with a few drops of essential oils.

I have tried both treatment options, and I have had both work for me. I also almost always have to take antibiotics when I get mastitis, so take that information and do what you believe would work best for you.

YEAST INFECTION IN THE BREAST (NIPPLE THRUSH)

Yes, this is a real thing. Once again, I learned this the hard way.

A yeast infection in the breast is also known as nipple thrush. A few ways you can get this include taking too many antibiotics, getting bacteria from the baby, hormonal changes that create a wet environment, poor hygiene, and improper cleaning of breastfeeding equipment.

Signs of nipple thrush include:

- Redness or swelling
- Tenderness or burning when nursing
- Itching, blisters, or white spots.

Treatment typically requires an antifungal ointment or, in some cases, oral medication prescribed by a doctor. Sanitize everything that comes into contact with the breast and the baby's mouth. Air out the breasts and keep them clean and dry.

If not treated soon enough, nipple thrush can cause mastitis. I can testify that yeast infections can cause mastitis and can be painful.

OVERSUPPLY

Oversupply occurs when you produce more milk than your baby needs. Too much pumping or nursing can cause this, along with genetics and hormones. Treatment may include less frequent feedings, feeding on one side only, reducing the number of pumping sessions or pumping time, and consulting a lactation consultant to determine the best course of action for your situation.

PRAYER DECLARATIONS

I decree my baby latches deeply and properly on my breasts.

My baby latches, feeds well, and empties my breasts.

My nipples will not crack or suffer adverse effects from nursing.

My breasts will produce the proper amount of milk for my baby.

My breasts are flowing with milk for my baby.

My milk drains properly and does not cause infection, blockages, or bacterial growth.

Clogged ducts cannot exist in my body.

My breast tissue is normal.

I pray my body has the correct amount of beneficial bacteria.

No bacteria can attack me, in Jesus' name.

I rebuke any yeast infection from coming forth.

My breasts will have no inflammation or infection, in Jesus' name.

There will be no redness or streaking on my skin.

I rebuke swollen, hot, painful breasts.

I bind and rebuke flu-like symptoms and fatigue.

Antibiotics will not have an adverse side effect on my body, in Jesus' name.

Mastitis will not negatively affect my milk supply.

I command mastitis to leave, in Jesus' name.

Section 10

Babies

Chapter 36

Meconium

Meconium is a baby's first poop. It's thick, black, and tar-like. It's made from things the baby ingested while in the womb. So yes—we, (Lauren) and you, are going to be talking about poop.

Meconium is normally passed after birth, but if it is passed in the womb, it's called meconium aspiration and can cause breathing problems. If a baby swallows some meconium, that is usually okay. When a baby inhales meconium, complications can arise.

Passing meconium after birth means your baby's digestive system and intestines are working properly.

Your baby's poop will slowly start to look less like meconium as they drink colostrum or take a bottle.

PRAYER DECLARATIONS

My baby will not be under stress or have a lack of oxygen during labor and delivery.

I command my baby's intestines not to overmature with gestational age and release into the stool.

I forbid my baby from passing meconium into the amniotic fluid before birth.

I proclaim my baby will not inhale and aspirate the meconium into his/her lungs before, during, or right after delivery.

I rebuke and take authority over Meconium Aspiration Syndrome. My baby will not inhale the meconium.

My baby will breathe easily and have clear airways.

I bind and restrict lung inflammation and infection.

There will be no respiratory distress, low oxygen levels, air trapping, or need for breathing assistance. My baby has the breath of life, (Genesis 2:7).

I command my baby's heart rate to be optimal; there will be no slowing of the heart rate during labor or delivery.

Chapter 37

Jaundice

Jaundice is a common condition in newborns caused by a buildup of bilirubin, a substance produced when red blood cells break down. During pregnancy, the fetus constantly produces and breaks down red blood cells. When this happens, bilirubin is produced. Because the fetal liver is still immature, it cannot process bilirubin efficiently on its own. Instead, bilirubin is transported through the placenta to the mother, where the mother's liver processes and eliminates it.

After birth, the baby no longer has the placenta to help remove bilirubin, and the newborn's liver may take time to catch up. When bilirubin builds up faster than the baby's liver can process it, it can cause jaundice, which shows up as yellowing of the skin and eyes.

Jaundice is often treated with simple, effective methods such as special light therapy, biliblankets, frequent feedings, and, in very mild cases, limited exposure to sunlight.

PRAYER DECLARATIONS

I call forth an easy delivery with no bruising, no vacuum needed, and no extra bilirubin released. My delivery will go forth in divine order and protection. My delivery will be great!

I say any blood type incompatibility that my baby and I may have will not cause higher bilirubin levels. The blood of Jesus covers any incompatibility in the natural, (Exodus 12:13).

As red blood cells break down, I decree that the liver can handle their processing and expulsion.

The liver will mature, process, and remove bilirubin from the blood.

My baby has good feeding skills and a normal number of bowel movements, so bilirubin is eliminated through the stool.

I thwart any jaundice in my baby. Bilirubin, you are normal, in Jesus' name.

Chapter 38

Colic

You bring this beautiful baby home, and it's supposed to be a wonderful, amazing time—finally getting to hold your little baby in your arms that you carried for nine months—but instead it's filled with frustration and tears. You're asking God for patience and peace every day.

Colic is when a baby who is well fed cries for three or more hours at a time for multiple days a week. This definitely described my experience, from 3 p.m. to 11 p.m., my baby cried. We tried everything: going for walks, going for car rides, gas drops, holding the baby, playing with the baby, more feedings, more frequent burpings—there was nothing we could do to make the baby stop crying.

We had friends and family come and hold the baby to give us a break, but for six weeks, all the baby did was cry most of the day. It was hard and definitely made it challenging to connect with this new baby I had just brought into the world, but we made it through it. There is no definitive known cause of colic, but we will pray over what we know can cause it.

PRAYER DECLARATIONS

I pray against any birth trauma my baby may have experienced.

I pray off any side effects from medicine and drugs during labor and delivery.

I command my baby to eat correctly. He/she will not swallow too much air while he/she is eating.

I declare my baby burps easily.

I rebuke that my baby has excess gas.

I pray over my baby's digestive system and say it processes food correctly and easily without gas.

I proclaim my baby processes milk and dairy well and adequately, in Jesus' name.

I decree my baby will not be sensitive to dairy. He/she will process breastmilk, formula, and milk well.

I speak over his/her nervous system and command it to regulate properly.

I speak to my baby and say, "You will adjust to life outside the womb with ease and peace."

I pray that no stress in my life will affect my baby. My baby is covered in the peace and joy that the Lord brings.

My baby sleeps well. He/she falls asleep easily on his/her own and is getting the proper amount of sleep he/she needs.

I pray peace over our house and everyone in it.

God, give me peace and patience to get through this season.

Holy Spirit, please show me what I can do to help my baby get over colic.

THINGS TO TRY:

- Go for a walk.
- If you can't walk far, push the stroller back and forth in your living room.
- A different terrain. My baby liked walking in the grass; it was a little bouncy.
- Go for a car ride.
- Gas drops.
- Facial massage.
- Babies can be overtired, and it appears as colic.
- If you are getting to your end and need a break but don't have anyone to take the baby, place the baby in a crib or bassinet and walk to the other end of the house for a few minutes. It is better for you and the baby to find a minute of peace while the baby is in a safe environment.

Section 11

Pregnancy Development
40 Weeks of Declarations

WEEKS 1 AND 2 – CONCEPTION

Conception occurs when sperm fertilizes an egg inside the fallopian tube. It typically happens two weeks after the last menstrual period.

PRAYER DECLARATIONS

I declare that the egg will receive the right sperm and that both will be healthy and strong.

I declare that each parent contributes 23 normal chromosomes to form the zygote (the first cell) when the egg and sperm fuse.

I declare that there are no chromosomal abnormalities (no extra, missing, or broken chromosomes).

There will be healthy accurate cell division with no chromosomal errors or DNA mutations.

Healthy DNA must transfer without errors during fertilization.

I declare that the egg will be in the fallopian tube at the perfect time to be fertilized by the sperm.

The egg will travel through the fallopian tube and form a blastocyst (a cluster of rapidly dividing cells that will become a baby and placenta), so it can implant into the uterine wall.

I declare that the sperm will reach the fallopian tube and meet the egg.

WEEKS 3 AND 4 - IMPLANTATION BEGINS

The fertilized egg travels through the fallopian tube to the uterus and attaches to the uterine lining. Once implantation occurs, the embryo begins to grow, and the placenta and amniotic sac begin to form.

The uterine lining must be thick, nutrient-rich, and free from inflammation or infection. Strong implantation also establishes early blood flow between the mother and embryo.

PRAYER DECLARATIONS

I declare that implantation will take place.

I declare that my uterus will accept the fertilized egg and support it, in Jesus' name.

I declare that the fertilized egg will pass through the fallopian tube with ease and will properly attach to the uterine lining.

I declare that the uterine lining is healthy, in Jesus' name.

I say that the fertilized egg is now attached to the uterine lining, in Jesus' name.

I declare that the embryo will begin to grow once it attaches to the uterine lining.

I declare that the placenta will develop properly.

I declare that the amniotic sac will form perfectly, in Jesus' name.

WEEK 5 – EARLY ORGAN FORMATION

The neural tube begins to form. It will become the baby's brain, spinal cord, and backbone. Small limb buds that will develop into arms and legs start to form. The heart and lungs begin to grow, and the heart starts to beat.

PRAYER DECLARATIONS

I command the neural tube to form properly and be healthy, in Jesus' name.

I command it to form perfectly into my baby's spinal cord, brain, and backbone.

I declare that the baby's heart begins to develop, with every part forming in perfect working order.

I command the baby's lungs to develop and function properly.

I declare that my baby will have a strong heartbeat and will continue to beat throughout his/her life.

WEEK 6 – FACIAL DEVELOPMENT AND HEARTBEAT

The heart is now beating. Basic facial features begin to form, including the mouth, nose, and ears. Fingers and toes start to form, and blood cells begin to develop. By this time, the brain consists of three regions: the forebrain (thinking and problem-solving), the midbrain (visual/auditory processing), and the hindbrain (coordination, balance, and heart rate).

PRAYER DECLARATIONS

I declare my baby's heart is beating and functioning perfectly.

I declare that my baby will have ten fingers and toes, with five on each hand and foot. Every bone, muscle, and ligament forms properly.

I declare that my baby's nose and ears grow and form perfectly.

I declare that blood cells are growing and forming perfectly, in Jesus' name.

I declare that the brain receives proper nutrients and develops properly, including the forebrain, midbrain, and hindbrain.

WEEK 7 – BONE, EYELID, BRAIN, GENITAL FORMATION

Bones are beginning to form, eyelids are developing, and the brain continues to mature. The genitalia begin developing.

PRAYER DECLARATIONS

I command every bone to develop properly. The baby receives the right amount of calcium and vitamin D for strong bones.

I pray that my baby's eyelids are developed.

I pray for protection over my baby's brain as it continues to develop, and that every part is forming fully, soundly, and according to God's perfect design.

I command my baby's genitals to develop properly and be in working order, in Jesus' name.

WEEK 8 – MAJOR ORGANS DEVELOP

All major organs and systems are beginning to develop. The placenta becomes functional. Eyes become visible, ears form, and the umbilical cord is fully formed and begins transferring blood and oxygen. Nerves develop, and the lungs begin to form.

PRAYER DECLARATIONS

I command that every organ is developing perfectly and functioning properly, in Jesus' name.

I command the placenta to function well, efficiently transferring nutrients and waste.

I command the placenta to produce the hormones needed to support this pregnancy fully.

I command the placenta to provide the perfect amount of oxygen and nutrients to my baby.

I declare that each eyelid and ear continues to form perfectly.

I declare that the umbilical cord forms correctly and transfers nutrients properly, in Jesus' name.

WEEK 9 – BABY ENTERS FETAL STAGE

Major organs continue maturing, and the baby rapidly increases in size and weight. Teeth start forming, taste buds develop, and muscles strengthen.

PRAYER DECLARATIONS

I say right now that my baby's teeth are forming properly, in Jesus' name.

My baby's taste buds are developing, in Jesus' name.

Every muscle in my baby's body is developing and forming according to God's perfect word.

My baby will have strong, fully functioning muscles, in Jesus' name.

WEEK 10 – LIMBS AND EXTERNAL FEATURES

Fingers and toes are now fully formed. Fingernails and toenails begin developing. Heart tones can be heard at prenatal appointments. The external genitalia and the ears continue to form.

PRAYER DECLARATIONS

My baby has ten fingers and ten toes, with five on each hand and five on each foot, in Jesus' name.

Every finger and every toe have nails growing as they should, in Jesus' name.

My baby's heart will beat strong and healthy, in Jesus' name.

The external genitals of my baby are forming correctly.

Each ear is forming perfectly. My baby will have excellent hearing, in Jesus' name.

WEEK 11 – MOVEMENT AND BLOOD CELLS

Baby begins opening and closing the mouth and fists. Knees, elbows, and ankles move. Bones harden. Red blood cells start to form to carry oxygen and carbon dioxide.

PRAYER DECLARATIONS

Every joint in my baby's body is fully functioning, in Jesus' name.

I declare that my baby's bones are hardening and strengthening in perfect alignment with the word of God.

My baby's mouth, fists, knees, elbows, and ankles are working correctly.

The red blood cells in my baby are forming perfectly, and the correct number is present in my baby's body.

WEEK 12 – ORGAN SYSTEMS ARE WORKING

Organs, limbs, muscles, and bones are formed and continue to grow. The circulatory, digestive, and urinary systems are working. The liver produces bile. The fetus drinks and expels amniotic fluid. Nerves allow the hands to open and close and to perform sucking movements.

PRAYER DECLARATIONS

Every organ, limb, muscle, and bone of my baby is continuing to grow according to the word of God.

I say that circulatory, digestive, and urinary systems are functioning properly. The liver is producing bile, in Jesus' name.

The baby's intestines are formed and are inside the abdomen.

The baby's nerves are working and telling the baby to open and close his/her hands.

WEEK 13 — VOCAL CORDS AND HEAD PROPORTION

During this week, your baby's vocal cords begin forming, and the head starts coming into better proportion with the rest of the body. It is part of God's design as the body develops in balance and order.

PRAYER DECLARATIONS

My baby's vocal cords are forming, in Jesus' name.

My baby will have no speech delays, in Jesus' name.

My baby will start talking at the correct developmental age.

Baby, your head and body are becoming beautifully proportioned.

Baby's vocal cords are forming correctly, in Jesus' name.

My baby will begin talking at the right time and have clear, healthy speech.

My baby's head and body are growing in proper proportion to each other, in Jesus' name.

WEEK 14 – SKIN THICKENING AND EARLY HAIR GROWTH

Your baby's skin begins to thicken, early hair growth starts, and the baby begins moving their hands toward their mouth and turning their head.

PRAYER DECLARATIONS

My baby's skin is thickening and preparing for life outside the womb.

My baby's hair is growing and getting thicker, in Jesus' name.

I will not have heartburn as a side effect, in Jesus' name.

My baby brings its fingers to its mouth and turns its head, just as God has created it to do.

WEEK 15 – ORGAN POSITIONING AND EARLY MOVEMENTS

Some organs, such as the intestines and ears, move into their permanent places. Baby practices breathing with amniotic fluid and begins making purposeful movements, such as sucking or smiling.

PRAYER DECLARATIONS

Baby, your lungs are strong and healthy. They are growing perfectly. They will be fully developed by the time you are born.

I say my baby is practicing breathing and building strong, healthy lungs.

I declare my baby is already smiling and happy and starting to make purposeful movements.

I declare my baby's pancreas and liver are starting to produce secretions.

WEEK 16 – HEARING AND LIGHT SENSITIVITY

Your baby's lips and ears are developed, the baby can hear, and the baby begins responding to light.

PRAYER DECLARATIONS

Thank you, Jesus, that this baby has two ears to hear and lips to speak.

I say that his/her ears and eardrums are forming in alignment with the word of God and that his/her lips are developing perfectly.

WEEK 17 – FAT DEVELOPMENT AND VERNIX COATING

Baby begins storing healthy fat and develops a protective vernix caseosa coating over the skin.

PRAYER DECLARATIONS

I speak life, health, and growth over my baby right now. As this baby grows, he/she will gain the proper amount of fat he/she needs to survive outside the womb.

I pray that vernix is covering my baby and protecting them from the amniotic fluid.

WEEK 18 – HAIR AND SLEEP RHYTHMS

Baby begins growing lanugo (a soft layer of hair) for warmth, forms early sleep-wake patterns, and may respond to loud noise.

PRAYER DECLARATIONS

Baby, you will have peaceful sleep, and your sleep cycle is already starting to be regulated.

Lanugo is forming on my baby's body, helping to keep them warm.

WEEK 19 – STRENGTH, MOVEMENT AND FINGERPRINTS

Baby becomes stronger, movement increases, hiccups may start, and fingerprints form.

PRAYER DECLARATIONS

Baby, you are growing healthy and strong. How joyous it is to feel you kick and punch.

Baby, your fingerprints are unique to you. God has designed them just for you.

WEEK 20 – NAILS FORM AND THE FIVE SENSES BEGIN TO DEVELOP

Baby's nails are growing, and the area of the brain that will help process the five senses is starting to develop.

PRAYER DECLARATIONS

Baby, your nails are growing strong and perfectly, in Jesus' name.

I declare that all five of your senses are developing properly, in Jesus' name. Touch, smell, taste, hearing, and seeing are all developing perfectly, in Jesus' name!

WEEK 21 – LIMBS MOVE TOGETHER, AND BLOOD CELLS ARE PRODUCED

Baby's arms and legs move more in sync, and bone marrow begins to help produce blood cells.

PRAYER DECLARATIONS

As your limb coordination develops, I declare that every movement works together fluidly and properly, in Jesus' name.

I pray that the baby's bone marrow is healthy and produces strong, healthy blood cells!

WEEK 22 – GRASP STRENGTHENS AND RESPONDS TO SOUNDS

Baby can grasp, touch its ears and the umbilical cord, and hear your heartbeat, stomach, and breathing.

PRAYER DECLARATIONS

Baby, you are getting stronger every day. You can grasp and touch things.

As you grow in my womb and hear me breathing and my heart beating, I pray it's comforting for you. I pray it brings you peace and comfort, inside and outside the womb, and that God will help me keep my emotions in check, so you only feel love and peace.

WEEK 23 – BABY ADDS BODY FAT

Baby rapidly begins to add body fat for warmth and strength.

PRAYER DECLARATIONS

I declare my baby is growing.

I declare that my baby is gaining the proper amount of body fat, in Jesus' name.

WEEK 24 – LUNGS MATURE FOR BREATHING

Baby's lungs are developing and preparing for breathing after birth.

PRAYER DECLARATIONS

I declare that my baby's lungs are fully developed.

My baby has strong lungs.

My baby will breathe the breath of life, Jesus Christ.

I thank You, Lord, that the breath of God goes with my baby.

WEEK 25 – MORE BODY FAT AND NERVOUS SYSTEM GROWTH

Baby continues to gain body fat, and the nervous system continues to develop.

PRAYER DECLARATIONS

My baby is putting on the proper amount of body fat, in Jesus' name.

My baby's nervous system is developing perfectly.

The vagus nerve is going to work perfectly every day of his/her life.

WEEK 26 – SKIN AND EYE COLOR DEVELOP, AND LUNGS PREPARE FOR LIFE OUTSIDE

Baby makes melanin for skin and eye color, and lungs begin producing substances needed for breathing.

PRAYER DECLARATIONS

I declare that melanin is being formed. I declare that your eyes are being formed into the beautiful color that God has planned for them to be.

I declare that your lungs will be ready for life outside of the womb at the time of birth. They are starting to make surfactant that will help you breathe after birth.

WEEK 27 – EYES OPEN AND EYELASHES FORM

Baby can open and close its eyes and has formed eyelashes.

PRAYER DECLARATIONS

My baby has 20/20 vision.

My baby can open his/her eyes and blink.

My baby's eyelashes are formed.

I thank You, Lord, for beautiful baby eyes that will sparkle and shine with Your love.

WEEK 28 – BABY TURNS HEAD-DOWN AND NERVES CONNECT

Baby begins turning head-down for birth, and nerves continue to connect and strengthen.

PRAYER DECLARATIONS

I speak to my baby and my body, and I say you are starting to prepare for delivery and birth.

Baby, you are turning head-down and face-down. You will stay that way through delivery.

Baby, your nerves are continuing to develop strongly and efficiently.

WEEK 29 – BRAIN DEVELOPS MORE RAPIDLY

A baby's brain goes through a season of quick growth and development.

PRAYER DECLARATIONS

I declare my baby's brain is growing in perfect alignment with the word of God.

Every neuron, cell, muscle and every part of his/her brain is made perfect and whole, in Jesus' name!

WEEK 30 – BODY TEMPERATURE AND BRAIN CONTINUE TO MATURE

The baby begins to regulate body temperature, and the brain continues to develop.

PRAYER DECLARATIONS

Baby, you can regulate your body temperature. Your body will have great circulation, in Jesus' name!

I pray the blood of Christ over my baby's brain!

Baby, you will be smart and capable, and you will be able to do anything you set your mind to.

WEEK 31 – BABY STORES MINERALS AND PATTERNS FOR SLEEP

Baby starts storing iron, calcium, and phosphorus and settles into more regular sleep–wake patterns.

PRAYER DECLARATIONS

Baby, you are almost here! As you continue to grow, you store iron, calcium, and phosphorus, helping prepare you for life outside the womb. Your sleep patterns will be more regulated, and you will sleep through the night after you are born.

WEEK 32 – ORGANS ARE FORMED AND STRENGTHENING

Most organs are formed and continue to develop and strengthen throughout life outside the womb.

PRAYER DECLARATIONS

Every organ and cell in my baby's body is formed properly and made strong, in Jesus' name!

Every organ is strong, complete, and free of defects. You will function properly.

WEEK 33 – BONES STRENGTHEN WHILE THE HEAD STAYS SOFT FOR BIRTH

Baby's bones harden while the skull stays soft and flexible for delivery.

PRAYER DECLARATIONS

I pray over my baby's bones, and I say you are strong and healthy.

The head will form as intended, remaining soft and flexible until birth, then will come together, harden, and form properly after birth.

WEEK 34 – PROTECTIVE COATING THICKENS

The creamy protective coating on the baby's skin thickens to prepare for birth.

PRAYER DECLARATIONS

I declare that the vernix thickens to help prepare you for birth, in Jesus' name!

WEEK 35 – BRAIN GROWTH CONTINUES

Baby's brain continues to grow and mature.

PRAYER DECLARATIONS

Brain, you will grow properly, in Jesus' name! You will receive the correct nutrients you need to develop well, in proper portions for baby's body, in Jesus' name!

WEEK 36 – HAIR DEVELOPS ON THE BABY'S HEAD

Baby loses most of the lanugo and begins growing hair on the head.

PRAYER DECLARATIONS

I pray that your hair follicles start to grow and that you will have healthy, full, and beautiful hair!

WEEK 37 – BABY SETTLES INTO THE PELVIS FOR BIRTH

Baby drops into the pelvis and moves into position for delivery.

PRAYER DECLARATIONS

Baby, I say you are dropping into my pelvis head down and face down. I declare that you are coming into the birth canal and will stay there till delivery. I declare that your shoulders and hips are in perfect alignment for delivery, in Jesus' name.

WEEK 38 – BABY GAINS FINAL WEIGHT

Baby continues to gain about half a pound a week and fine-tunes body systems.

PRAYER DECLARATIONS

I declare my baby is gaining half a pound a week.

Thank You, Jesus, that all the major systems of my baby are fully developed and ready to live life outside the womb.

WEEK 39 – FULL TERM

Baby is considered full term and ready.

PRAYER DECLARATIONS

Thank You, Jesus, that my baby is full term and created perfectly in Jesus' name.

WEEK 40 – DUE WEEK

Baby is ready to be born in God's perfect timing.

PRAYER DECLARATIONS

I pray in the mighty name of Jesus that these prayers and declarations have been answered. I pray that my baby is made perfect and whole in God's wonderful image. I pray that any part of my baby that I may have forgotten to pray over has developed perfectly, in Jesus' name. Thank You, Jesus, that I have made it to 40 weeks. I pray that, as we prepare for labor and delivery, You will be with us. I pray that You are continuing to watch over this baby and help them grow perfectly and have a strong and happy life, in Jesus' name. Amen.

Closing Message

We are praying for live births and healthy children. Unfortunately, we don't always get what we pray for. We have faith, we pray, but it doesn't always happen. I am a firm believer that God does not cause sickness, death, chromosome errors, deformed babies, etc. It says in the Bible that the thief comes to steal, kill, and destroy, and that the Lord has come to give us life and have us live it abundantly, (John 10:10).

I believe if a baby is born with physical limitations or congenital disabilities, it is the enemy, environmental factors, medications (which are manufactured), or some trauma or health issue that happened to mama. However, I refuse to believe that something God, our Father, made in His image, (Genesis 9:6) is imperfect. God would not do that. He would not need to for His glory, or so He could have another "little angel" in heaven. Children are people, made in God's image. He doesn't take them from us because He needs another little angel in heaven.

However, terrible things do happen, and often children die or are born with birth defects. What I do believe firmly and am experiencing in my own trials as a grandma is that God causes all things to work together for His good, (Romans 8:28). In 2024, we had a medically complex grandson born into our family with a rare syndrome and chromosome deficiency. I have sought the Lord for answers and have really studied this Scripture to find that answer. Do I believe God caused it? Absolutely not! Do I believe my grandson will be healed of multiple brain and body deficiencies and diagnoses? Absolutely, I do!

What I have learned from this Scripture is that it doesn't necessarily mean all things are working for our good, but that it is for His good. Even when we can't see it or believe it, we are called to live by faith, not by sight, and our story is for His glory. When people are truly living to serve the Lord, they will take the test or the trial and turn it into a testimony for the good of helping others. They will find a way to redeem the lost by implementing a program, business, or ministry to help others. Therefore, in the end, all things are truly working for the good of those who love God and have been called according to His purpose. This life is temporary! Whatever we endure now is but for a moment. I am sorry for your loss, your pain, and for your child that didn't turn out the way you expected. I've had a miscarriage, infertility, a C-section, vaginal birth, a NICU baby, a failure-to-thrive child, and now a grandson diagnosed with moderate brain abnormalities affecting his entire body and life. Despite all of that, I refuse to give in to defeat! I will never allow the enemy to steal the joy or the moments I have now with my three living children, four grandchildren, and one in the womb!

I have learned through being healed 17 times without medical intervention (see my book, *Healed at Last*) that my story is not my story alone. It is my story for His glory, and my story can change your story. I would never have written *Healed at Last* and reached so many people if I hadn't had one of those Romans 8:28 moments in my personal life. Have hope. We serve a God of hope. Our prayer is that you truly experience life and life abundantly. Our grandson, Noah, is alive. And even though he has several complications to overcome, my saying is, "As long as he is alive, God can heal him." Stay strong. Keep believing and receive all God has for you.

About the Author-Kathy DeGraw

Kathy DeGraw is passionate about physical healing, prayer, and helping people overcome mental battles. Having personally experienced divine healing from the Lord seventeen times, she is driven to equip others with faith-filled understanding to receive and believe for healing. As an author, speaker, podcaster, and television host, Kathy carries a deep burden to see people both physically and spiritually healed through prayer and discipleship.

As the founder of Kathy DeGraw Ministries and K Advancement LLC, she ministers with boldness, releasing the love and fire of the Holy Spirit while teaching believers how to walk in the fullness of God and activate their prophetic potential. The Holy Spirit has been her best friend, and Kathy delights in imparting to others how to live led by the Spirit.

Kathy hosts the podcast and television program *Prophetic Spiritual Warfare*, airing on ISN and podcast platforms. She has also been featured as a guest on *The Jim Bakker Show* and Sid Roth's *It's Supernatural!*

Kathy is married to her best friend, Ron DeGraw, and they reside in Michigan. It is the joy of her life to be a mom and grammy.

To schedule an interview or a speaking engagement visit kathydegrawministries.org.

Find us on social at Kathy DeGraw.

About the Author-Lauren DeBoer

Lauren DeBoer is a devoted wife and mother who enjoys life on the farm, riding horses, and spending time with her family and friends. She has faithfully served on a worship team for thirteen years and has traveled worldwide with her mother, sharing the gospel and ministering to others.

After walking through pregnancy and experiencing complications firsthand, Lauren developed a deep desire to support and encourage other women on their pregnancy journeys. Through her own experiences, she has witnessed the powerful fruit of prayer and prophetic declaration, both during her pregnancies and through the home declaration book she authored. Lauren is passionate about helping women strengthen their faith, stand on God's promises, and find hope and confidence throughout pregnancy and motherhood.

Contact Lauren by email at ldeboer.kdministries@gmail.com.

Additional books by Lauren DeBoer & Kathy DeGraw include:

Prayer Declarations for Your Home: *Powerful Declarations for Buying, Selling & Spiritually Protecting Your Home*

Additional books by Kathy DeGraw include:

Healed at Last: *Overcome Sickness and Receive Your Physical Healing*

Mind Battles: *Root Out Mental Triggers to Release Peace*

Unshackled: *Breaking the Strongholds of Your Past to Receive Complete Deliverance*

Prophetic Spiritual Warfare: *Partnering With the Holy Spirit to Manifest Your Destiny*

Discerning and Destroying the Works of Satan: *Your Deliverance Guide to Total Freedom*

Spiritual Warfare Declarations: *Prayers that Break Strongholds and Release Healing*

Speak Out: *Releasing the Power of Declaring Prayer*

Activate Your Faith with Anointing Oil: *Biblical Usage and Understanding of Anointing*

www.ingramcontent.com/pod-product-compliance
Lightning Source LLC
Chambersburg PA
CBHW071433090426
42737CB00011B/1649